BRADSHAW
AT THE SEASIDE

John Christopher and
Campbell McCutcheon

AMBERLEY

Left: George Bradshaw. As a young man he was apprenticed to an engraver in Manchester in 1820, and after a spell in Belfast returned to Manchester to set up his own business as an engraver and printer specialising principally in maps. In October 1839, Bradshaw produced the world's first compilation of railway timetables. Entitled *Bradshaw's Railway Time Tables and Assistant to Railway Travelling*, the slender cloth-bound volume sold for sixpence. By 1840 the title had changed to *Bradshaw's Railway Companion* and the price had doubled to one shilling. It then evolved into a monthly publication with the price reduced to the original sixpence. This volume is the latest in the Amberley series of books based on *Bradshaw's Descriptive Railway Hand-Book of Great Britain and Ireland*, which was originally published in 1863.

About this book

This book is intended to encourage the reader to explore many aspects of the railways of Britain. Through Bradshaw's account and the supportive images and information it describes some of the many changes that have occurred over the years. Hopefully it will encourage you to delve a little deeper when exploring the railways and other works, but please note that public access and photography of the railways are sometimes restricted for reasons of safety and security.

First published 2015

Amberley Publishing
The Hill, Stroud
Gloucestershire, GL5 4EP

www.amberley-books.com

Copyright © John Christopher and Campbell McCutcheon, 2015

The right of John Christopher and Campbell McCutcheon to be identified as the Author of this work has been asserted in accordance with the Copyrights, Designs and Patents Act 1988.

ISBN 978 1 4456 4382 3 (print)
ISBN 978 1 4456 4409 7 (ebook)

British Library Cataloguing in Publication Data.
A catalogue record for this book is available from the British Library.

Typeset in 9.5pt on 12pt Celeste.
Typesetting by Amberley Publishing.
Printed in the UK.

Beside the Seaside

> Railways may now be considered as accelerators of pleasure as well as of business, bringing as they do the most favourite watering places along the coast within the compass of a brief and agreeable journey. Of these mediums of transit, we know of few more inviting to the tourist than the one we are about to describe, passing as it does, through a succession of the most varied and diversified scenery, fraught with a host of welcome associations, and terminating at a sea-side town, which fashion in persuit of pleasure has justly selected for a marine residence.

As this excerpt clearly demonstrates, Bradshaw – or at least the company which produced the guidebooks in its founder's name as George Bradshaw had died in 1853 – appreciated the significance of the railways redefining many of Britain's coastal towns. However, the Bradshaw guides were also playing their part shaping the travelling habits of the British public and, in particular, popularising the use of the railways for leisure.

This is the latest volume in the Amberley series of books based on *Bradshaw's Descriptive Railway Hand-Book of Great Britain and Ireland*. Universally referred to simply as 'Bradshaw's Guide', it is the guidebook that featured in Michael Portillo's *Great British Railway Journeys*. By the time that the first guide had appeared on the bookstalls in 1863, the railways had lost their pioneering status and, with the heady days of the railway mania of the 1840s over, they were settling into the daily business of transporting people and goods. Within its densely typeset pages

Below: A traditional seaside scene of children building sand castles at Blackpool, *c.* 1910.

Above: A *Punch* cartoon on the perils of bathing machines. 'I want you to take my friend here and myself just far enough to be up to our chins, you know, and no further!'

it is possible to find many references to the growth of the 'watering places', the little harbours and working coastal towns that were to experience enormous and sudden growth in the ensuing fifty years as the British discovered the pleasures of the seaside. In some cases small settlements mushroomed into major towns and Bournemouth, which barely gets a mention from Bradshaw, is a good example of this phenomenon.

The material for this survey of seaside destinations is organised differently to the previous books in the series. This is because the Bradshaw guides invariably took the reader on a linear railway journey from A to B. As a result, the coastal towns are usually at the end of such journeys, and there are only a couple of instances where the lines actually follow the coast itself, such as in the Brighton area and on the South Devon Railway. Therefore, starting with London – and a great many railway journeys and excursions did and still do – we head eastwards down the Thames estuary into northern Kent and follow the coast, county by county, in a clockwise direction, continuing along the Channel, up the Bristol Channel, and so on. Inevitably there is greater coverage of some areas than others and, in some cases some surprising omissions. This reflects several factors: the extent of the railway network at the time and the subsequent development of some seaside resorts. Bradshaw's viewpoint is inevitably London-centric and the South East in particular is well covered: it could be visited by a new breed of day-trippers from the capital. Other areas had yet to emerge as leisure destinations and Cornwall, for example, is dismissed by Bradshaw as 'one of the least inviting of the English counties'.

This then is a view of the British seaside seen through Victorian eyes. A time when entertainment was to be found in bathing-machines, health-giving waters, fresh air and a well-stocked municipal reading room.

Kent

This county forms the south-eastern extremity of the island of Great Britain, bounded on the north by the Thames; on the east and south-east by the German Ocean and the Straits of Dover; on the south-west by the English Channel and county of Sussex; and on the west by that of Surrey.

From the diversity of its surface, the noble rivers by which it is watered, the richness and variety of its inland scenery, and the more sublime beauties of its sea coast, this county may be said to rank among the most interesting portions of our island; while the numerous remains of antiquity, the splendid cathedrals, venerable castles, and mouldering monastic edifices, are connected with some of the most remarkable events in English history.

Two chains of hills, called the Upper and Lower, run through the middle of the county from east to west, generally about eight miles asunder; the northern range is part of the extensive ridge which runs through Hampshire and Surrey to Dover, where it terminates in the well known white cliffs. Beyond the southern or lower range is what is called the Weald of Kent, a large tract of rich and fertile land. Kent is essentially and almost solely an agricultural county. The Isle of Thanet is remarkably fertile, but in the Isle of Sheppey only one-fifth of the land is arable; the rest consists of marsh and pasture land, and is used for breeding and fattening sheep and cattle. The Thames, the Medway, the Stour, the Rother, and the Darent are the principal rivers; while numerous streams diffuse fertility in every direction.

SOUTH EASTERN RAILWAY

By means of the SER the watering places on the coast of Kent, viz., Gravesend, Margate, Broadstairs, Ramsgate, Deal, Dover, and Folkestone, can be reached in a few hours; and the inhabitants of the metropolis are thus enabled to enjoy the advantages of a visit to the sea-side at their favourite towns, the climate, temperature, and atmosphere of which many prefer and find more beneficial than that of the watering places on the South Coast.

WHITSTABLE

Distance from station, ¼ mile. A telegraph station.

HOTELS – Two Brewers; Bear and Key.

OMNIBUSES to and from the station; also to Faversham.

FAIR – Thursday before Whit-Sunday. MONEY ORDER OFFICE at Whitstable.

WHITSTABLE is the harbour of Canterbury, and is celebrated for its oyster fishery, the produce of which, under the name of natives, is highly esteemed in the London and other markets. The town, though rather mean in appearance, and irregularly built, has a bustling and thriving appearance, from its fishing and coal trade,

Herne Bay
Above: The clock tower on the busy prom at Herne Bay.

Margate
Right: The Lifeboat Statue on the Marine Terrace at Margate was erected in 1899 to commemorate the sinking of the vessel *Friends to All Nations* two years earlier.
Below: Margate Jetty. Like many of Britain's early piers, it played an important role as a landing stage for the pleasure steamers. It was destroyed by a storm in 1978.

LIFEBOAT STATUE, MARGATE. 118. *Marine Series*

HERNE BAY

Distance from Sturry station, 6 miles. A telegraph station.

HOTELS – Pier, and Dolphin. OMNIBUSES to and from Sturry station, thrice daily. MARKET DAY – Saturday. FAIR – Easter Monday.

HERNE BAY, so named from the old village of Herne, about a mile and a half distant, which was thus called from the number of herons frequenting the coast at this point, was not twenty years ago more than a scanty collection of houses, irregularly built along the beach. It has now become a fashionable and somewhat populous watering-place, with long lines of streets, many of them still unfinished, stretching out in every direction. In 1831, a pier from one of Telford's designs was commenced, and now presents an elegant and substantial structure, extending 3,640 feet over the sands and sea. At the extremity are commodious flights of steps for the convenience of small vessels and passengers landing at low water, and a fine parade sixty feet in width and upwards of a mile in length has been formed on the adjoining shore. The air is very bleak but invigorating, and the sea purer, it is considered, than at Margate. A considerable portion of the adjacent land, and the very site of the town itself, was anciently covered by the waves, constituting the estuary which admitted the passage of the largest vessels, and divided the Isle of Thanet, from the mainland. Mrs Thwaites, the widow of a wealthy London merchant, has proved a munificent benefactress to the town, for, in addition to having built and endowed two large charity schools, she has caused to be constructed also a clock tower, which serves the purpose of a lighthouse as well. A new church has been built in the centre of the town, with a chapel of ease and a dissenting chapel, and there is also an infirmary for boys from the Duke of York's military school at Chelsea. On the Parade is a large bathing establishment, with an elegant assembly-room adjoining, to which apartments for billiards, reading, etc., are attached. Libraries and bazaars also been recently introduced in the usual number and variety. The old village church, with its embattled roof and square tower, is a spacious edifice, comprising a nave, two aisles, and three chancels.

MARGATE

POPULATION, 8,874. Distance from station, ½ mile. A telegraph station.

HOTELS – Gardner's Royal; White Hart.

STEAMERS to London daily in summer, thrice weekly in winter.

MARKET DAYS – Wednesday and Saturday.

MONEY ORDER OFFICE at Margate. BANKERS – Cobb & Co.

There is not, in the whole range of our sea-side physiology, a more lively, bustling place than this said Margate: albeit, by those who are fettered down to cold formalities, and regard laughter as a positive breach of good-breeding, it is pronounced to be essentially and irredeemably vulgar. The streets are always a scene of continued excitement, and troops of roguish, ruddy-cheeked urchins, escorted by their mammas or their nursery-maids, traverse every thoroughfare about the town from morning until night. There is a theatre also, and a kind of minor Vauxhall, called the *Tivoli*, where those who care little for out-of-door enjoyments can spend a passable hour in such dramatic and musical gratifications as the artists and the place can best afford. Bazaars and marine libraries afford too, in 'the season', the latest metropolitan vocal novelties; and the same raffling and rattling of dice-boxes to test fortune's favouritism, is carried on as at Ramsgate, but with a greater spirit of freedom and earnestness. In short, for those who do not go to the coast for retirement, and who like to have an atmosphere of London life surrounding them at the sea-side, there is no place where their desires can be so easily and comprehensively gratified as here.

The increasing extent and importance of the town makes one regard the traditions told of its early origin as being nearly akin to the fabulous, yet a few centuries back, known to the local chroniclers as coeval with the period of 'once-upon-a-time', Margate was a small fishing village, with a few rude huts thrown up along the beach, and having a *mere* or stream flowing at that point into the sea, whence it derived its present appellation. When London folks, however, grew wiser, and found that short trips had a wonderful power in preventing long doctors' bills, the place grew rapidly into repute, and the old Margate – immortalised by Peter Pinder – disgorged its hundreds of buff-slippered passengers annually. Since then steam has done wonders, and Margate visitors have to be numbered by hundreds of thousands in the same space of time. The only drawback to its salubrity, as a place of residence is that a cold cutting north-easterly wind is frequently encountered, and not being sheltered by a range of hills, the effect on an invalid of delicate constitution is of rather an injurious tendency than otherwise. But this apart, the air is keen, fresh, and invigorating, and, with persons in good health, will have a material influence in keeping them so. It is generally a few degrees cooler in July and August than Ramsgate.

The sixth day of April, 1810, saw the commencement of the present pier, and five years afterwards it was finished from a design by Rennie, and at a cost of £100,000. It is nine hundred feet in length, sixty feet wide, and twenty-six feet high. A day ticket for one penny will not only give admission to the promenade, but afford an opportunity besides of hearing a band perform for a few hours in the evening. There is a lighthouse at the extremity, which is an elegant ornamental Doric column as well, and was erected in 1829. At an expenditure of £8,000 the well-known Jarvis's Jetty was constructed in 1824, out of the finest old English oak that could be procured. It extends 1,120 feet from the shore, and forms a pleasant cool promenade when the tide is out, although a scurrilous wag has compared it to walking along an excessively attenuated cold gridiron. The Clifton Baths, by the Fort, cut out of the chalk cliffs, are unquestionably the most commodious, and have some interesting appendages in the shape of a library, winding passages, curious vaults, daily newspapers, and an organ. The other bathing-houses, though well conducted, are of a more ordinary character.

Margate being situated partly on the acclivities of two hills, and partly in the valley below, the streets partake of that tortuous and undulating character which is so much pleasanter to look at than to climb. On the Fort, in front of East-crescent, the handsome structure of Trinity church is conspicuously situated, and to the south-east the old parish church of St John occupies a similarly elevated position. In this latter there are some curious old tombs and monumental brasses that should not be forgotten. A literary and scientific institution is supported by the annual subscriptions of the inhabitants, and has a library, lecture-room, and museum, that may vie with any out of London.

Extending about a mile along the shore there is a stout barricade of stone, erected as a defence to the incursions of the sea, at an outlay of £20,000. The sum £4,000 more rebuilt the Town and Market Place in 1821; and from this it be seen that the townsfolk have not been chary of their coin in contributing to the security and embellishment of their native place. Inns and hotels of every grade are scattered in and about the town with prodigal luxuriance, and lodging houses are everywhere. The staple manufacture of the landladies here may be set down as – beds.

The visitor should not neglect to make a pilgrimage to the old Roman station of Reculver and Richborough, the ruins of the old castle of the latter being still in a state of tolerable preservation. Races are held on the downs, by Dandelion, in the middle of September, and generally attract a large concourse of spectators.

Two images reflecting the changing attitudes to public bathing in the sea. *Right:* A Bamforth postcard, 'Guess which are my knees – the fat wobbly ones,' wrote its sender in Brighton, 1963. *Below:* The Victorians were more modest as shown by *Punch.* 'Seaside puzzle – to find your bathing-machine if you've forgotten the number.'

HERE WE ARE AGAIN—BOW LEGS, HAIRY LEGS, FAT LEGS, KNOCK-KNEES (CAN YOU PICK ME OUT?)

I'M WELL HOOKED AT RAMSGATE.

Ramsgate

Above: The harbour, inner basin. As Bradshaw puts it, Ramsgate was 'little better than a fishing village before the close of the century'.
Left: 'I'm well hooked in Ramsgate.' These Bamforth postcards would be over-printed with a variety of locations. *Below:* A colorchrom view of the sands, *c.* 1895.

RAMSGATE

POPULATION, 11,865. A telegraph station. HOTELS – Royal; Royal Albion; Royal Oak. MARKET DAYS – Wednesday and Saturday.

FAIR – August 10th, at St Lawrence. MONEY ORDER OFFICE at Ramsgate.

BANKERS – Branch of the National Provincial Bank of England. Burgess & Son.

RAMSGATE was little better than a mere fishing village before the close of the last century, and all the noble streets and terraces stretching seaward are the growth of the present. Its prosperity has been literally built on a sandy foundation, more permanent than the adage would teach us to believe, for the sands, which are really unequalled for extent, were long the prominent attraction of visitors. In 1759 was commenced the pier, built chiefly of stone from the Purbeck and Portland quarries, involving an expenditure of nearly £600,000. This stupendous structure affords an excellent marine promenade of nearly three thousand feet in length. The form is that of a polygon, with the two extremities about two hundred feet apart. The harbour comprises an area of nearly fifty acres, and can receive vessels of five hundred tons at any state of the tide. The first object that arrests attention at the entrance to the eastern branch of the pier is the obelisk, fifty feet in height, which commemorates the embarkation of George IV from here on his Hanoverian excursion in 1821. The next is a tablet, at the octagonal head, setting forth the name of the engineer and the dates of the erection. Opposite is the lighthouse, casting at night a brilliant reflection over the dark waste of waters, and forming a striking feature in the scenery of the coast. Far away, like a phosphoric gleam upon the channel, is the floating beacon called 'the Gull', which, with two smaller ones near Deal, becomes visible after dusk from the pier. Eight seamen and a captain, who has only occasionally a month's leave of absence, are entrusted with the management of the beacon, and in this desolate and dangerous region they are doomed to battle with the elements at all seasons, cheered alone by the reflection that through their vigilance thousands are perhaps annually preserved from the perils of shipwreck. The Goodwin sands, traditionally said to have been the estate of earl Godwin, father of King Harold, form the roadstead called the Downs, and extend from the North Foreland to Deal, but as they are continually shifting under the influence of the winds and waves, their exact locality can never be ensured.

Nowhere is the accommodation for bathers more perfect than at Ramsgate, whether the green bosom of the Channel be selected for a plunge, or a private bath chosen instead. Most of these establishments, where baths can be had at all hours, are elegantly fitted up with hot air stoves, luxuriant ottomans, and refectories and reading-rooms adjacent. A communication with the upper portions of the town, built upon the high range of cliffs, is formed by two convenient flights of stone steps, called Augusta Stairs and Jacob's Ladder. The lawny esplanade that has been formed before the crescents facing the sea enables a promenader to obtain an ample sea view, and the Downs being continually studded with shipping, the picture is generally extremely varied and animated. Some elegant churches in the florid Gothic style, and numerous places of dissenting worship, are to be met with

LONDON BRIDGE STATION.

Left: London Bridge Station, the main departure point for steam trains to the South East.

Middle left: Another lost form of transport, the SRN hovercraft operated by Hoverlloyd from the grandly sounding Ramsgate International Hoverport. It merged with Hoverspeed in 1966 and ceased operations in 1981.

Broadstairs
Below: The railway did not reach the town until 1863, hence its omission in Bradshaw's guide.

10,260. - BROADSTAIRS

in convenient situations about the town, and in Harbour-street is the new Town Hall, erected in 1839, with a capacious market underneath, teeming with every kind of comestible of various degrees of excellence.

Boarding-houses, hotels, and dining-rooms are in the usual watering-place abundance, and the limits of expenditure may be adjusted to the depth of every purse. The bazaars and libraries provide evening amusement in abundance, through the agency of music and raffles; and though the books partake of the elder Minerva press school of composition, and the raffling is generally for articles of indifferent worth, the excitement attendant upon both is quite sufficient for sea-side denizens.

No one of course would think of stopping a week at Ramsgate without going to Pegwell Bay, where the savoury shrimps and country-made brown bread and butter are supposed to have been brought to the very highest degree of perfection. And for a quiet stroll in another direction there is Broadstairs, two miles to the north-east, very genteel and very dull; the aspect of this 'exceedingly select' place of residence being so imposingly quiet as to make one involuntarily walk about on tip-toe for fear of violating the solemn sanctity of the place. It is, however, a very agreeable excursion for a day, and an excellent plan is to go by the path across the cliffs, past the elegant mansion of Sir Moses Montefiore, and return by the sands at low water. The old arch of York gate, built by the Culmer family in the reign of Henry VIII, is the sole vestige of the once extensive fortifications that bristled up at the back of the old quay. There was a pier, too, swept away by the terrific storm in 1808, which destroyed that of Margate, but the rough wooden substitute is not the less picturesque, and there is a fine wholesome odour of sea-weed about the old rugged rafters, enough to make one willing to forego the fashionable for the fragrant. A mile beyond is Kingsgate, where Charles II landed, and furnished a pretext for endowing it with a regal title. Another mile, and the North Foreland lighthouse, 63 feet in height, may be reached, and entered too, if the curious visitor will disburse a small gratuity to the keeper. It is well worthy of inspection.

DEAL

POPULATION, 7,531. Distance from station, 1 mile.
A telegraph station. HOTEL – Royal. MARKET DAY – Saturday.
FAIRS – April 5th and October 10th. MONEY ORDER OFFICE at Deal.
BANKERS – Branch of the National Provincial Bank of England.

This town stands close to the sea shore, which is a bold and open beach, being defended from the violence of the waves by an extensive wall of stones and pebbles which the sea has thrown up. The sea opposite the town, between the shore and the Goodwin Sands, is termed the Downs. This is about eight miles long and six broad, and is a safe anchorage; and in particular quarters of the wind, as many as 400 ships can ride at anchor here at one time. Deal was formerly a rough-looking, irregular, sailor-like place, full of narrow streets, with shops of multifarious articles termed slops or marine stores. It is however being much improved, and is now

Dover

Although thought of more as a port than a seaside resort nowadays, Dover had its day as a 'watering-place' in Bradshaw's time. *Above:* The railway tunnel through the Shakespeare Cliff, between Dover and Folkestone.

Left: An advertising postcard for the 'most interesting town on the south coast'. It offers sea bathing as well as Turkish and medical baths.

Below: Big lady, small donkey.

resorted to for sea bathing, especially on account of its good repute for moderate charges. The bathing establishment at Deal is well conducted, and there are good libraries.

It is a great pilot station for the licensed or branch pilots of the Cinque Ports; the Deal boatmen are as fine, noble, and intrepid a race of seamen as any in the world, and as honest as they are brave. *Deal Castle* is at the south end of the town.

The village of **Walmer** is a detached suburb of Deal, towards the south on the Dover Road. Since Her Majesty resided here, Walmer has been much unproved and extended. It now contains several handsome villas, inhabited by a large body of gentry. The air is very salubrious, and the surrounding country pleasant and agreeable. *Walmer Castle*, one of the fortresses built by Henry in 1539, is the official residence of the Lord Warden of the Cinque Ports. It is surrounded by a moat and drawbridge. The apartments are small but convenient, and command a splendid view of the sea; but they will always have a peculiar interest for Englishmen, as having been the residence of the Duke of Wellington, and at which he died in 1852.

Sandown Castle is about a mile to the north of Deal; it consists of a large central round tower, and four round bastions with port holes, and on the sea-side it is strengthened with an additional battery.

From Minster to Ramsgate the line is on a tolerably steep incline. Kent and the Kentish coast have long been celebrated for their delicious climate and exquisite pastoral scenery, and the railway passes through a fine panorama of marine and picturesque views, until it reaches...

DOVER

POPULATION, 25,325. A telegraph station.

HOTELS – The Ship; The Lord Warden; The Gun.

POST HORSES, FLYS, etc., at the hotels.

BOATS to mail packets when outside harbour, fare, 2s each person.

PORTERAGE of luggage to packets and station, 1s to 1s 6d, each person.

COACH to Walmer and Deal, four times daily.

STEAMERS to Calais, Boulogne, and Ostend, daily, except on Sundays.

MARKET DAYS – Wednesday and Saturday. FAIRS – November 23rd, lasting over three market days, and Charlton Fair in July.

MONEY ORDER OFFICE. BANKERS – National Provincial Bank of England.

This much frequented point of continental embarkation has of late years occupied a prominent position among the watering-places of our island. The line of continuous terraces of noble-looking mansions spreading along the margin of its coast, the pureness of its atmosphere, the bold and rocky headlands that distinguish its marine scenery, all contribute to give it an important position among the recently created destinations of our sea-loving citizens. The associations, too, that cling to the white cliffs of Albion – not, as of yore, frowning defiance to our Gallic neighbours, but with a better spirit illuminating their weather-beaten features with sunny smiles of welcome – all tend to draw every year crowds of fleeting visitors to a spot so renowned in song and story. It has been well said, that scarcely any great man, from King Arthur to Prince Albert, has failed, at some period or other, to visit Dover, and all history confirms the assertion. Divided from the French coast by a passage of only twenty miles across the British Channel, Dover is advantageously situated on the margin of a picturesque bay, sheltered by the promontory of the South Foreland, and screened by its lofty cliffs from the piercing northerly winds.

Ancient as Dover is as a town and port, it is, as we have said, comparatively modern as a watering-place. In 1817, houses were commenced on the Marine Parade, and, about the same period, Liverpool Terrace, and the contiguous lawns, Guildford and Clarence, were projected, followed, in 1838, by the noble mansions of Waterloo Crescent and the Esplanade. These form, in conjunction with others, a continuous range of imposing buildings that extend nearly from the Castle cliff to the north pier. Close to the sea is the Promenade, which, during the summer season, presents a complete galaxy of beauty and fashion, not infrequently enlivened by the performance of military music. The facilities afforded to bathers merit great commendation, and the clear transparency of the water is not the least of the advantages here derived.

If not the most elegant thoroughfare in Dover, Snargate Street is decidedly the most picturesque. With the towering white cliffs on one side, and a row of excellent shops on the other, it presents a contrast that seems to link agreeably the permanent majesty of the past with the fleeting characteristics of the present. Here is situated the Post Office, nearly opposite to Rigden's library, the theatre, the Apollonian Hall, in which concerts are frequently given, and a bazaar, which affords a pleasant lounge for those who like to court the smiles of fortune in a raffle. Adjoining the Wesleyan Chapel, also in the same street, is the entrance to the grand military shaft leading to the heights and barracks above. The communication is by an arched passage and a vertical excavation, having three spiral flights of 140 steps each. The barracks are sufficiently capacious to contain many thousand troops; and beyond, following the military road, we come to the grand redoubt, occupying the site of an ancient Pharos, the ruins of which are called Bredenstone, or the 'Devil's Drop'. Nowhere will the tourist find more extensive and beautiful views than a promenade at sunset on these heights will afford. Westward is the town of Boulogne, with its lofty column to commemorate an invasion which never took place; eastward, rising as it were from the ocean, is the white tower of the Hotel de Ville, and the revolving phare of the town of Calais. Turn which way we will there is something to admire. On one side is the magnificent Castle, still rearing its stately battlements in majestic grandeur, after braving the blasts of a thousand winters, and bringing back to the eye of the imaginative beholder the by-past glories of the days of chivalry; on the other, the noble cliff an object sufficiently striking from its own native sublimity, but rendered doubly attractive and interesting to every spectator by its association with the greatest work of our greatest bard. Perhaps in the whole circuit of the kingdom there is not another spot so calculated to awaken in the bosom of an Englishman feelings of pride and exultation, as the objects around call up in succession reminiscences of those martial and intellectual achievements by which the inviolate island of the sage and free has attained her present unquestioned supremacy amongst the nations of the world. An evening stroll on these picturesque heights will amply repay the trouble of the ascent.

[Bradshaw describes the section of line to the west of Dover, as seen on a train travelling from Folkestone to Dover.]

After leaving Folkestone, the traveller will encounter the most wonderful portion of the line. The rapidity of our progress is such as to allow but little time, however, for examination of the extraordinary engineering works and achievements. Prepared by a shrill shriek of the whistle, we plunge into the Martello tunnel, and then, scarcely with a breathing interval, enter the second or Abbot's Cliff tunnel. Emerging from this, the line continues along a terrace supported by a sea wall for nearly a mile, and presenting a delicious scenic contrast with the marine expanse that opens to the right. This brings us to the Shakespeare Cliff tunnel, double arched for greater security, on escaping from which, an embankment raised from the shingle again receives us, and darting through the sturdier excavation of Arch-cliff Fort, we are brought, with varied sensations of dreamy wonder and delight, beneath the elegant terminus at Dover. The viaduct on the Dover side is also considered fine work; it is about half a mile long, and formed of heavy beams of timber securely framed and bolted together, but left open so as to offer less resistance to the waves in bad weather.

FOLKESTONE
  POPULATION, 8,507. A telegraph station.
  HOTELS – Pavilion; Royal George; Clarendon.
  OMNIBUSES to and from the station; also to Sandgate, Ashford, Canterbury.
  POST HORSES, FLYS, etc., at the hotels.
  STEAMERS – To Boulogne, twice daily in the summer, in two hours, and once in the winter.
  MARKET DAY – Thursday.
  BANKERS – Branch of the National Provincial Bank of England.

FOLKESTONE is rapidly becoming a much frequented watering place, as well as a favourite point of embarkation to France; the distance to Boulogne is only twenty-seven miles, and the voyage generally accomplished in two hours and a half. The opening of the South Eastern Railway, and the establishment of a line of packets between this port and Boulogne, has been the means of rescuing Folkestone from its previous obscurity, and bringing it to its present position. It is situated on the side of a range of hills on very uneven ground, the streets are narrow, steep, and irregular, and the sea-worn chasms about the shore seem still to perpetuate in appearance that reputation for contraband traffic which once was its distinguishing feature. The air is very salubrious, and has been thought of much

Folkestone

Left: The Victoria Pier opened in February 1888. It was damaged by fire in 1945 and the remains lay derelict until final demolition came in 1954. *(LoC)*

Above: Two of the less saucy comic postcards; these were published by Bamforth and by D. Constance.

Left: The Wandering Players, photographed in Hythe in 1906.

efficacy in nervous debility, whilst the country round is highly picturesque, and abounds in varied and beautiful landscapes. Visitors here may enjoy all the benefits of sea bathing and sea air, with more retirement than at Dover or Ramsgate.

Folkestone Hill is 575 feet high, and commands a beautiful prospect of the town and adjacent country, through which the railway is seen winding its devious course. To those who do not mind a little pedestrianism, and who delight in formidable ascents and footpaths trembling on the brink of ocean, we can conscientiously recommend a walk across the cliffs to Dover, which besides presenting a succession of romantic scenery will be found to afford some advantageous opportunities for inspecting the shafts connected with the ventilation of the railway tunnels running underneath.

Sandgate, a small watering place two miles from Folkstone, has been much frequented within the last twenty years by invalids, who wish for quiet and retirement. It has several detached villas, and the roads between Folkestone and Sandgate, either along the shore or over the cliff, are exceedingly picturesque and romantic. Sandgate Castle is of great antiquity. The country around is highly interesting, and abounds in beautiful views and landscapes, ruined castles, and other remains of olden times.

HYTHE

HOTEL – White Hart. A telegraph station.

HYTHE lies 3½ miles to the south of Westenhanger Station, easily accessible by omnibuses that meet the trains.

The town of Hythe is small, but clean and healthy, and prettily situated at the foot of a hill extending down to the sea. It is beginning to be resorted to by visitors, for whom accommodation is provided on reasonable terms. The church on the hill has a light tower, ornamented by four turrets. It is one of the Cinque Ports. Near Hythe commences Romney Marsh, extending along the coast for twenty miles, and including about 60,000 acres, which within the last few years have been successfully drained and cultivated.

The deep chalk cutting that succeeds our departure from Westenhanger introduces us to Saltwood Tunnel, and, emerging from this, we immediately catch on the right the first transient glimpse of the sea – that sight which involuntarily quickens our pulse, and sends a pleasurable emotion tingling through our veins. A lofty amphitheatre of hills, stretching away in the blue distance, varies the view in the opposite direction. Then comes an embankment, and, borne across a viaduct 90 feet above the valley below, we come almost magically within a fine view of Folkestone and its harbour.

"THAT'S MY OLD MAN JUST COMING UP, ALICE!"
"BY GUM, HE'S GOT A RED FACE!"
"NAY, LASS, PUT YOUR SPECS ON!"

Above: LBSCR loco departing from Victoria station for the South Coast.
Left: Bamforth card posted in 1946.
Below: Yachts launching in Hastings, *c.* 1895. *(LoC)*

Sussex

One of the Southern Counties, varied by the inequalities of the Downs and by intervening vales, to which the wooded scenery and pasture land give a rural and a rich diversity of appearance. It belongs to the chalk formation, and has some high ranges of downs and hills. The north is occupied by the *Wealden* formation, covering 420,000 acres, and the south by the chalk formation. On the east are marshes and alluvial lands, and on the west coast it is much indented by, at others it runs out into, bold cliffs.

This county is celebrated for its breed of sheep, which are fed on the South Downs, the name by which they are distinguished. This, and the adjoining counties of Hants and Surrey, were by the Romans denominated Belgae, from the circumstance of their being inhabited by a people called Belgians, who supplanted the British Celts.

The railway communication of the county of Sussex is supplied by the London, Brighton & South Coast Railway Company (LBSCR). The London and Brighton main line, commencing at the London Bridge Terminus, proceeds past Sydenham and Croydon to Reigate, thence enters the county of Sussex at Crawley, and passes due south to Brighton, having branch lines extending along the coast to Lewes and Hastings, and Newhaven to the north, and to Shoreham, Worthing, Arundel, Chichester, Havant, and Portsmouth on the south.

The London and Brighton railway is 50½ miles in length, and traverses a considerable portion of the counties of Surrey and Sussex.

The Brighton Company was the first to commence running excursion trains, which are now provided by most of the other companies throughout the United Kingdom, as affording a profitable source of revenue to the companies, and being the means of 'popularising' the towns, localities, and scenery in connection with the respective lines.

Railways may now be considered as accelerators of pleasure as well as of business, bringing as they do the most favourite watering places along the coast within the compass of a brief and agreeable journey. Of these mediums of transit, we know of few more inviting to the tourist than the one we are about to describe, passing as it does, through a succession of the most varied and diversified scenery, fraught with a host of welcome associations, and terminating at a sea-side town, which fashion in pursuit of pleasure has justly selected for a marine residence.

WINCHELSEA

Distance from station, 1½ mile. A telegraph station. HOTEL – New Inn.
PASSENGER VANS to Hastings. MARKET DAY – Sat. FAIR – May 14th (Cattle).
MOTEY ORDER OFFICE at Rye.

The original sea port, which bore its name, was swallowed up by the sea on the eve of St Agatha, 1287, and although the buildings were then erected further inland, the sea, unappeased by the former sacrifice, broke in anew, and finally, in the time of Queen Elizabeth, altogether choked up the harbour. The ruins of the castle of Camber, built by Henry VIII, are still standing, and so are three out of the four town gates, but they are in a ruinous condition.

HASTINGS

POPULATION, 22,910.

A telegraph station. HOTELS – The Marine, on the Parade; Albion; Castle.

OMNIBUSES to and from the station to meet every train.

POST HORSES, FLYS, etc., at the hotels and station, to meet every train.

MARKET DAYS – Saturdays (corn); daily (poultry).

FAIRS – Whit Tuesday, July 26 and 29, and November 27.

The recognised salubrity and mildness of the air, together with the openness of the coast and the smoothness of the beach, have long made Hastings a favourite and a recommended resort. The shore is not abrupt, and the water almost always limpid, and of that beautiful sea-green hue so inviting to bathers. The constant surging of the waves, first breaking against the reefs, and next dashing over the sloping shingle, is not unwelcome music at midnight to the ears of all who *sleep* in the vicinity of the shore. Dr James Clark states, that in winter Hastings is most desirable as a place of residence during January and February:

During the spring also it has the advantage of being more effectually sheltered from north and north-east winds than any other place frequented by invalids on the coast of Sussex. It is also comparatively little subject to fogs in the spring, and the fall of rain may be said at that time to be less than on other portions of the coast. As might be expected from the low and sheltered situation of Hastings, it will be found a favourable residence generally to invalids suffering under diseases of the chest. Delicate persons, who desire to avoid exposure to the north-east winds, may pass the cold season here with advantage. Owing to the close manner in which this place is hemmed in on the sea by steep and high cliffs, it has an atmosphere more completely marine than almost any other part of this coast, with the exception, of course, of St Leonards, which possesses the same dry and absorbent soil.

The breadth and extent of its esplanade, also, and the protection afforded by the colonnades for walking exercise, are circumstances of considerable importance to the invalid, and render a conjoined residence at Hastings and St Leonards a very efficient substitute for a trip to Madeira.

The Castle of Hastings, for a time the favourite residence of the Conqueror, has remained a mass of magnificent ruins; its towers, bastions, and ancient walls forming an object truly picturesque, as seen from any point of view, but looking even grand in their sombre desolation, as meeting the eye of the pedestrian when ascending the eminence leading to Fairlight Downs.

A few years back the visitors to the castle were shown *two* coffins, a small one and a larger one, which they were assured contained the ashes of mother and infant. These have been lately removed, and the space of ground enclosed by the walls which used to shelter such vestiges of a more barbarous age is now employed by a market gardener to administer to the culinary wants of the townsfolk of Hastings and St Leonards.

The approach to Hastings Castle is from the further extremity of Wellington Square, and, with the perpendicular cliff that fronts the sea for its base, the outer walls appear originally to have had the form of a triangle with rounded angles. For some time past the interior has been laid out as a flower garden and shrubbery, and the person who has charge of the lodge accommodates, for a small fee, visitors with seats and refreshments. The view, though not equal to that from Fairlight Downs, is varied and extensive, and commands towards the south an ample marine expanse, whilst Beachy Head, Eastbourne, and Bexhill may be seen towards the west.

Whilst in the neighbourhood, it should not be forgotten that a delightful excursion may be made to Battle Abbey, not more than six miles distant. The grounds are now in possession of the Webster family, who have liberally thrown them open to public inspection every Friday, at 1½ p.m. It is here that the 'Battel Roll', a sort of primitive 'Court Guide', is carefully preserved, and furnishes a list valuable to the antiquary and historian of those families who came over with William the Conqueror.

A glance into the booksellers' windows, where engraved vignettes of some neighbouring attraction allure the eye in every direction, will at once reveal to the visitor the tempting beauty of the environs. A week may be delightfully spent in exploring the fairy-like nooks about Fairlight alone. Situated in a sweet umbrageous spot, down which, by narrow winding steps, hewn out of the solid rock, one only can descend at a time, is the weeping rock. The view of this constantly-dripping well, as the spectator looks up to the jutting rock from the beautiful cottage of Covehurst below, is well calculated to inspire the mind with that feeling under which credence would be given to any legend that accounted for this freak of nature, by ascribing it to the influence of supernatural agency. The stone weeps, as it were, from myriads of pores, and, although the water falls in continuous drops, no trace of it is left in the reservoir; passing through the rock, its appearance is as mysterious as its disappearance is magical. It is explained by the soil beneath being loose and sandy, over a heavy beach stone foundation, and, acting as a subterraneous drain, the water is conducted beneath the surface, appearing as a truculent stream about a hundred yards from the rock, and then again disappearing down a declivity. The beautiful appearance the rock presents in winter, when the drip is frozen and the icicles hang from the sloping crags in clusters of crystals, will not be easily forgotten by those who have had the good fortune to witness, at this period, such a mimic stalactite cavern.

Then, in the vicinity of the well are the fish-ponds with romantic walks around it, and a comfortable farmhouse adjacent, where refreshments can be had at a small cost, and where the ale is – but we forbear our eloquence. The picturesque

Hastings

Above: The East Cliff at Hastings before the coming of the cliff railway, which opened in 1903.

St Leonards

Left: The Marine Court building looks like an ocean liner and was completed in 1937 in the Streamline Moderne style, a later variation on the art deco theme much in favour on the South Coast.

Bexhill

Bottom left: A more traditional seafront look with the Sea Marina at neighbouring Bexhill.

waterfall of Old Roar should not be overlooked, nor the Lover's Seat, so charmingly enthroned amid shrubs and evergreens, nor the other favoured localities, which are enough to make a Pennsylvanian lawyer turn poetical. Let the pedestrian, however, make his way to the signal house belonging to the coast-guard station at that point, and he will have a panoramic view around him which it would be worth his while walking from Cornhill to Grand Cairo only to behold and then walk back again.

The whole forms a complete circle; the sweep of inland scenery extending to the hills in the neighbourhood of London, and the sea view reaching from Beachy Head to Dover Cliffs, between seventy and eighty miles apart, and stretching out to the heights of Boulogne. The entire area of the prospect, both by land and water, cannot be less than three hundred miles. Among many minor objects visible may be enumerated ten towns, sixty-six churches, seventy Martello towers, five ancient castles, three bays, and forty windmills. The best time for seeing it is the afternoon, when the setting sun lights up the old town of Hastings in the foreground, and brings into strong shadow the opposite coast of France. Upon favourable atmospheric influences it is, indeed, a view never to be forgotten.

ST LEONARDS

A telegraph station. HOTELS – Royal Victoria; Royal Saxon.
MARKETS – Daily.

ST LEONARDS, the recognised 'west-end' of Hastings, with which it is now connected, a fine noble archway marking the boundary of the two townships, was planned and executed by the well-known architect, Mr Decimus Barton, who only commenced his bold project in 1828. Hotels of eastern magnificence, public gardens, looking like realisations of the Arabian Nights' descriptions, libraries where the most fascinating novel gains an additional charm from the luxurious sea fronting ottomans, on which their perusal may be indulged, together with an esplanade peerless in its promenading conveniences – these are but a few of the manifold attractions which St Leonards holds forth to tempt the errant visitor into becoming a stationary resident.

On the hill, by the railway station, as you approach Bulverhithe, may be seen the ruins of the Conqueror's Chapel, supposed to mark the spot where he landed. Recent antiquaries have laboured to prove that it must have been nearer Pevensey.

BEXHILL

The village of which name is situated on a rising ground not far from the sea. It is a quiet, retired place, having some good iron springs, and is situated in a beautiful country.

Telegraph station at St Leonards, 3 miles. HOTEL – Bell.
FAIRS – June 28th, and 1st Monday in July.

Many persons prefer the retirement of Bexhill, with its fine bracing air, to the excitement and bustle of the neighbouring towns.

Just a line from
EASTBOURNE.

Eastbourne

Above: A charming early postcard from Eastbourne, together with a more recent photograph of the Central Bandstand with the pier in the background.

Brighton

Left: The station at Brighton. The arrival of the London & Brighton Railway, in 1841, brought hordes of day-trippers to the coast from London, and as a result the population grew from 7,000 in 1801 to 120,000 by 1901.

Littlehampton

Bottom left: A paddle steamer is towing a sailing barge in the harbour at Littlehampton, a 'small hamlet on the coast, which has some admirers as a retired watering place'.

The Pier and Harbour, Littlehampton

PEVENSEY

near the town of that name.

Telegraph station at Polegate, 3½ miles. HOTEL – Royal. MARKET DAY
– Thursday (Southdown Sheep). FAIRS – July 5th and September l5th.

Though formerly a place of so much importance as to give name to the hundred, it
has now dwindled to an inconsiderable village; and the sea, which formerly laved
the castle walls, has now receded to a distance of two miles. A number of Martello
towers, erected at the time of the last war – we hope the phrase will be just as
applicable for a hundred generations yet to come – remain as memorials of the
means resorted to for the defence of the coast.

EASTBOURNE

Distance from station 1 mile. A telegraph station.
HOTEL – Lamb. MARKET DAY – Saturday. FAIRS – March 12th and October
10th. MONEY ORDER OFFICE, at Eastbourne.

EASTBOURNE has, within a very few years, become fashionable as a watering-
place. The bathing is very good, and a number of machines are employed. It has
also the advantage of mineral springs, the waters of which are said to resemble
those of Clifton. A theatre, a ball-room, a library, and reading-rooms are the
principal attractions of the town, and there are good walks and rides. It lies about
three miles west of Beachy Head, is much recommended for its bracing air, and
offers the somewhat rare attractions of the beauty of country scenery and stately
trees, almost close to the sea. Eastbourne town lies about a mile and a half from
the beach or sea-houses, the actual watering place. The sea-houses comprise hotels,
lodging houses, baths, etc. Beachy Head on the right is a favourite excursion point.
To the left is the esplanade, and further inward the large circular fort of redoubts;
and in the distance several Martello towers. Eastbourne has one of the finest
churches in the country – Norman and early English.

BRIGHTON

POPULATION, 87,317. A telegraph station. HOTELS – The Bedford Hotel; Royal
York; Bristol; Old Ship; Pier; the Clarence, etc. OMNIBUSES to and from the
station and Hove every train, and Shoreham, daily. MARKET DAY – Tuesday
(corn), and Saturday. FAIRS – Holy Thursday, and September 4th. BANKERS
– The Brighton Union Bank; Hall, West & Co; London & County Bank.

The BRIGHTON TERMINUS is an elegant structure, fitted up in the most
convenient manner. There is a portico in the Roman architectural style, which
projects on pillars into the street, and is surmounted by an illuminated clock.

This once famous resort of royalty and fashion may now, through the literal as
well as metaphorical levelling of the railroad, be fairly entitled to the appellation
of the Marine Metropolis. Merchants who formerly made Dulwich or Dalston the

Brighton's Piers

Above and left: The Winter
Gardens and Brighton's
Palace Pier, built in 1899.
The earlier West Pier
was closed in 1975 and
badly damaged by fire in
2003. *Below:* The view
westwards from the pier.

boundries of their suburban residences, now have got their mansions on the south coast, and still get in less time, by a less expensive conveyance, to their counting-houses in the city. Excursions are now made with greater facility, and possibly more enjoyment, to Brighton, than would have, a few years back, sufficed for the common-place pilgrimage to Hampton Court; and a constant succession of trains, conveying a host of pleasure-seekers and business men to and fro, now traverse with marvellous frequency and precision the line that has sprung, by the magical enterprise of man, from tracts of waving corn-fields and boundless breadths of pasture.

About two miles from Brighton, Hollingbury Hill – no mean eminence of itself – stretches northward towards Lewes, and occupies a conspicuous position in the landscape. Before you is a majestic range of buildings – such as perhaps no other town in the kingdom can boast – sweeping down the sides of the cliff in every direction, and sheltering the three miles of architectural magnificence which forms the sea frontage, whilst beyond spreads the swelling sea, an object of such grandeur as in its ever-changeful expanse to outvie the lavish richness with which art has fringed its cliffs and shingled shores.

As will be at once apparent on descending the street leading from the station, the town is seated on an eminence that declines gradually towards the south-east, with a sloping undulation towards the Steyne, and then again ascends to the eastward. The twang of saltness that greets the lip, and the freshening, invigorating tone of the breeze, are agreeable proofs, on your first entrance, of the bracing bleak atmosphere that characterises the climate, though in various portions of the town, more sheltered, the air will be found adapted to the exigencies of the most delicate invalid. The panoramic view that first bursts upon the eye is so striking of itself, that it may be worthwhile glancing at it in detail, for the benefit of the visitor's future peregrinations.

To the left are seen two noble turfed enclosures, both thickly planted with shrubs, and laid out in the style of our metropolitan squares. The further section, intersected by a road, is the old Steyne, in the northern enclosure of which is Chantrey's bronze statue of His Majesty the fourth George, erected in at a cost of £3,000, collected among the visitors and inhabitants. This memorial crowns the square, and, as it were, points out the actual founder of the magnificence and prosperity of the place. The building which rises with domes and minarets, and is fretted with greater variety than taste, is – we cannot say how long it will remain – the Marine Pavilion of Her Majesty, erected for George the Fourth, after a fanciful oriental model, which, despite its supposed resemblance to the Moscow Kremlin, has had no precedent before or since. Adjoining are the royal stables, the main architecture of which is a vast glazed dome, lighting a circle of about 250 feet. It will be seen that the chief streets are not only wide and handsome, but well paved and brilliantly lighted, whilst the shops are of absolute metropolitan magnificence, with goods equalling in quality, and, on the average, not much excelling in price, the wares destined for a London sale. The profusion of squares, terraces, crescents, and steynes, with the bold beauty of the esplanade itself, produces a pleasing impression of variety, enhanced by the amphitheatre of hills that enclose the town beneath, and loom out in startling relief against the summer sky. The groups of animated nature identified at the corner of every thoroughfare, and the busy stragglers of the streets, are all of the marked watering-place description – pleasure seekers, out for the day, and eager to be ubiquitous, hurrying to and fro, through the market, to the spa, the race-course, the windmill, the beach, the shops, and the chain-pier, in as rapid succession as the most ingenious locomotion could devise. Then appear invalids, trundled out in bath chairs on to the Parade, to catch the earliest sunbeams; scores of laughing, chubby, thoughtless children, skilled manifestly in the art of ingeniously tormenting maids, tutors, governesses, and mammas; prawn-sellers and shell-fish hawkers a few, and flymen a multitude, all idly vociferating, whilst, intent upon their customary constitutional walk, the morning habitues of the promenade swing lustily past. Let us mingle with the throng, and obtain a closer intimacy with the principal features of the place.

Kemp Town – the most magnificent range of private dwellings in the kingdom – is on the estate of Thomas Read Kemp, Esq., of Black Rock, at the eastern extremity of Brighton, and is fronted by an esplanade, which is a delectable spot whereon to cultivate the intellectual. On a clear day the eye may reach from Beachy Head to the Isle of Wight, catching between the points many a bold outline of cliff and crag. The cliff here is 150 feet high, and the tunnel under the road, cut through the rock from the centre of the crescent lawn, is a very ingenious mode of shortening the distance to the lower esplanade. From Kemp Town a brisk walk over odoriferous downs brings us to Rottingdean, a village rather peculiar than either pretty or picturesque. It is famous chiefly for its wells, which are empty at high water, and full to overflowing at ebb tide. There is, however, an excellent inn for the accommodation of company, unexceptionable in the quality of its fare.

Returning past the old Steyne, we arrive opposite Mahomed's baths, in the busiest past of Brighton. Here we find fishermen mending their nets, boats laid up for repair, the fish-market and vendors engaged in every characteristic employment to be met with in a maritime town. Here also are pleasure-boats and sailing-vessels to be hired, where, if a party club together, a few hours' sail may be compassed for a dozen shillings. From here the Market Hall is but a short distance; it stands on the site of the old Town Hall, and was built in 1830. It answers every purpose in being spacious, unconfined, and well supplied daily with fresh and fine comestibles. The new Town Hall – a vast pile of building, with three double porticoes – cost £30,000, and has a handsome assembly-room an the upper story, rendered available for divers purposes of provincial legislation and amusement. A few, very few, years back, the battery was on the western verge of the town, and beyond it the several houses seemed to be fairly in the country. A quiet hotel or two, and a bathing establishment, reminded us that we were still in Brighton, and a solitary villa, belonging to the Countess St Antonio – a kind of Italianized cottage, with two wings, then the scene of many a gay rout notwithstanding its humility – just kept the fashion of the place in mind as, many a time and oft, we lingered on the rough and barren road to Shoreham, strewn with the flowers of hoar antiquity.

The line of extension has now become almost interminable, and most conspicuous in the elongation of the western esplanade is Brunswick-terrace, built from the designs of Mr Busby, a son of Dr Busby, of musical memory. The terrace consists of forty-two splendid houses, and has a very majestic aspect. Between the two great divisions of the frontal line lies Brunswick-square, open to the sea towards the south, and the whole is fronted by an artificial esplanade, which extends a mile in length. Along this delightful walk the votaries of fashion are wont to exercise their 'recreant limbs', and recruit their wasted energies with the invigorating sea-breeze.

The chain-pier, which has been for years entitled to the first consideration of the Brighton visitor, is well worthy of being still considered its greatest lion.

Hazlitt has said, 'there is something to being near the sea like the confines of eternity. It is a new element, a pure abstraction.' The mind loves to hover on that which is endless and ever the same, and the wide expanse which is here visible gratifies his feeling to the uttermost. The approaches to the pier are handsome and spacious, and the reading-room at the north end, with its camera above, is a delightful lounge for the promenader, who, having inhaled health by instalments of breathing, may therein plunge into the world of fiction, and enjoy a perusal of the last new novel with the zest of a marine atmosphere.

Churches, chapels, and meeting-houses, of all ages and for all denominations, are plentifully strewn over the town. The most modern is the handsome church of St Peter's, erected about twenty years ago, in the best pointed style, by Sir C. Barry, the well-known architect of the new Houses of Parliament. But the oldest, and perhaps the most interesting, is the ancient parish church of St Nicholas, standing on the summit of a hill at the north-west extremity of the town. It is an excellent sea and land-mark, and is said to be as old as the reign of Henry VII. From this pleasant locality the esplanade and parade are seen to much advantage. Gay loiterers of pleasure, and donkey parties, regiments of schools, and old bathing women, literary loungers, who read out of doors, and stumble against lamp-posts in interesting passages – these, and a host of other peripatetic humanities, make the beach populous between Hove and Kemp Town.

With regard to inns, taverns, hotels, lodging and boarding-houses, nowhere are they more numerous than here, their excellence of accommodation of course varying with price. Bathing establishments, too, are almost as numerous, whilst, for amusements, there is no provincial town in the kingdom that can offer such a variety of assembly and concert-rooms, libraries, bazaars, and other expedients for slaughtering of our common enemy – Time. In the New-road is the theatre – one of the prettiest out of London – and close adjoining is the Post-office, concerning which, in these economical days of epistolary communication, it may be as well to know the precise hours of dispatch and delivery.

The race-course is about a mile and a half north-ward of the town, on the summit of one of the loftiest and most commanding downs in the neighbourhood. The races generally take place early in August.

As the Brighton excursionist will go to the Devil's Dyke, as a matter of course,

JACK TAKES THE FAMILY FOR A ROW.

Worthing
Above: Bradshaw noted that the former fishing town had become a very fashionable watering place.

Bognor Regis
Below: The New East Parade. The town acquired the suffix of Regis relatively recently, in 1929, from George V who came to Bognor to convalesce after a serious illness.

we do not stay to tell him how he shall behold there from the Isle of Wight, spread beneath him like a map, or Beachy Head, looming like a snow-peak to the east, and the Downs far away, mingling with the horizon. But be it gently whispered, that on the margin of this demoniacal defile there standeth a small hostel, the glories of whose bread and cheese and ale have been sung by many an aristocratic voice. Everybody that ever was there assures you that for baking and brewing it stands unrivalled, although we shrewdly suspect that the preparatory course of Southdown oxygen has wonderful agency in appreciation of a fare so humble.

PORTSMOUTH BRANCH

Brighton to Worthing, Chiecester and Portsmouth

On leaving the terminus the line turns off abruptly towards the east, and passing through the New England tunnel, cut in the chalk cliff beneath Henfield Road, reaches the station of...

HOVE
Telegraph station at Brighton, 1 mile.

This village is now a suburb or continuation of Brighton. The old church of Hove is a fine edifice, and there is a new cross-shaped one, with a tall spire. There are fine walks here over the Downs. The summit of a high cliff in the neighbourhood, called the Devil's Dyke, is much visited for the fine views it affords of the surrounding country.
PORTSLADE and SOUTHWICK stations.

KINGSTON-ON-SEA
A telegraph station. HOTEL – Kingston Inn.
MONEY ORDER OFFICE at Shoreham.

This village is shunted on the right of the line; it has a harbour and wharf and is said to be prosperous and thriving. The line proceeds along the shore, presenting no feature worth remarking, until it reaches

NEW SHORHAM
A telegraph station. HOTELS – Surrey Arms; Buckingham Arms; and Swiss Cottage. MARKET DAY – Every alternate Monday (corn). FAIR – July 25th.

OLD SHOREHAM, on the right of the line, has a fine old Saxon church, which has been recently restored, and is much admired as a beautiful specimen of Saxon architecture.

NEW SHOREHAM is a borough town and a port, situated at the month of the River Adur, over which there is a suspension bridge. The harbour is about a mile to the eastward of the town.

LANCING STATION

In close proximity of the village of that name, known as Lancing-by-Sea, which is in some repute as a quiet, retired bathing-place, but it is excessively dull and *ennuyant.*

Telegraph station at Worthing, 2½ miles. HOTELS – Farmer's, and Sussex Pad.

After this we reach the more important station and town of...

WORTHING

POPULATION , 5,805. HOTELS – Sea House and Steyne. OMNIBUSES to and from the station. MARKET DAYS – Wednesday (corn), and Saturday. FAIR – July 20th.

This market town has lately become very fashionable as a watering-place. Its rise from an insignificant hamlet to its present rank has been rapid almost beyond precident, even in the annals of this coast. It is said to owe this distinction to the superior mildness of its temperature, arising from the shelter afforded by the Downs, which, at the distance of scarcely a mile, environ it, and exclude the chilling blasts of the northern and eastern winds, rendering bathing practicable even in the depth of winter. The climate is perhaps somewhat relaxing. The sands, extending nearly ten miles in length, are level, hard, and compact, and afford a beautiful ride or walk. Like Brighton, the town follows the line of the sea, the esplanade extending for three-quarters of a mile along the shore. Towards the close of a summer or autumnal evening no more delightful promenade can be imagined than this beach, as it echoes to the hollow murmuring of the waves, rippled with the sea breeze, whilst afar off can be gas-lights of the town of Brighton, forming a continuous chain of beads of light.

LITTLEHAMPTON

A short distance from a small hamlet on the coast which some admirers as a retired watering place.

BOGNOR

POPULATION, 2,523. Telegraph station at Woodgate, 1½ mile. HOTELS – York, and Norfolk. MONEY ORDER OFFICE.

BOGNOR is a pleasant bathing place, with good beach, crescent, etc., and much frequented, the air being very pure, and the situation delightful. It was made a market town in 1822 and owes its rise to Sir Richard Hotham, in 1985.

34

Hampshire

One of the southern counties of England, bounded on the east by Surrey and Sussex; on the south by the English Channel; and on the west by Wiltshire and Dorsetshire. It extends in length, from north to south, about fifty-five miles; in breadth, from east to west, about forty. The surface of Hampshire is beautifully varied with gently rising hills, fruitful valleys, and extensive woodlands. The chief part of the county is enclosed, though large tracts of open heath and uncultivated lands remain, especially in that part which borders Dorsetshire. The manufactures of Hampshire are not considerable; the principal are those of woollen goods. Great quantities of excellent malt are made at Andover; malt and leather at Basingstoke, also silk, straw hats, and paper; vast quantities of common salt, and of Epsom and Glauber salts, at Lymington; and in the neighbourhood of Redbridge there are valuable salt marshes. The minerals of Hampshire are scarcely deserving of notice, though the chalk strata and the rocks along the coast present very interesting objects to the geologist. Hampshire is much resorted to for the purpose of sea-bathing, and also as a fashionable summer residence, and bathing houses have, in consequence, been erected all along the coast. The scenery of the New Forest is particularly admired, and the whole county abounds with villas and country seats.

The railway communication of the county is supplied principally by the South Western Railway Company, from Farnborough Station to Winchester, Southampton, Portsmouth, Salisbury, etc., and the Great Western have a branch line between Reading and Basingstoke.

FAREHAM

POPULATION, 4,011. A telegraph station. HOTEL – Red Lion.
MARKET DAY – Tuesday. FAIRS – June 29th.
MONEY ORDER OFFICE at Fareham.
BANKER – Branch Hampshire Banking Company.

The trade of this place consists of coal, corn, canvas, and ropes. Much resorted to in the sea-bathing season.

GOSPORT

POPULATION, 7,789. A telegraph station. HOTEL – Crown.
OMNIBUSES to Anglesea and Alverstoke, daily.
STEAM BOATS to Ryde, Cowes, and Southampton.
MARKET DAY – Thursday. FAIRS – May 4th and October 10th.

GOSPORT, in the reign of Henry VIII, was merely a miserable village, inhabited by poor fisher-men, and its present importance may justly be ascribed to its convenient situation on the western side of Portsmouth harbour, and its contiguity

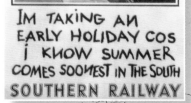

IM TAKING AN
EARLY HOLIDAY COS
I KNOW SUMMER
COMES SOONEST IN THE SOUTH
SOUTHERN RAILWAY

Top: Southsea's South Parade Pier from the air.

Middle left: The most famous of the Southern Railway's advertising posters, with a little boy talking to the engine driver at Waterloo.

Middle right: The Southampton-based ferry named after Gracie Fields.

Left: Aunt: 'It's very nice, I dare say; but I won't come any nearer to the cliff, for I am always afraid of slipping through those railings!'

to the Royal Naval Arsenal. The stores, fortifications, and long range of forts, all formed about the commencement of the present century, give a very forcible idea of the value attached to its commanding position; but the streets, narrow and dirty, have anything but a prepossessing appearance to a stranger. The ferry across the harbour, which is here nearly a mile broad, is contrived by means of the steam floating bridge, sufficiently capacious to convey vehicles as well as foot passengers across to Portsmouth, in a journey that rarely occupies more than eight minutes. The toll is one penny for each time of passing. About one mile north of Gosport, near Forton Lake, is the new Military Hospital, and at the extremity of that point of land which forms the western extremity of Portsmouth Harbour is Haslar Hospital, founded at the suggestion of Earl Sandwich, and completed in 1762. It is capable of affording accommodation to about 2,000 invalids. The average expenses of this establishment, intended exclusively for the reception of sick and wounded seamen, is about £5,000 per annum. The portico of the centre part of the building is surmounted by the royal arms, flanked by two figures personifying Commerce and Navigation. A new suburb, called *Bingham Town*, contains some genteel modern residences. The railway extends 1½ miles farther to...

STOKES BAY

At which point there is a floating bridge which conveys passengers from the railway across the Solent, to the Isle of Wight. The little village of *Anglesea*, close at hand, affords a miniature watering place for those among the residents who are not disposed to go further from home.

PORTSMOUTH

POPULATION, 94,709. A telegraph station.
HOTELS – The Fountain; the York; Pier. OMNIBUSES to and from the station; also to Waterloo and Petersfield. STEAM BRIDGE to Gosport every half hour.
MARKET DAYS – Thursday and Saturday. MONEY ORDER OFFICE.
BANKERS – Branch of the Bank of England; Grant, Gilliland & Long; National Provincial Bank of England.

PORTSMOUTH, the first naval port in the British Islands, and a parliamentary borough etc., 75 miles from London by the South Western Line, or 95 by way of the Brighton and South Coast Line. Within a short distance from Portsmouth, excursions may be made to the *Isle of Wight* and the following places: *Porchester Castle*, at the top of Portsmouth harbour, can be reached by boat (the pleasantest way, passing all the men of war), or by railway. From Havant, at the east end of Portsdown, looking down on Chichester Cathedral, there is a bridge to Hayling Island, a flat pasture tract like its neighbour, and separated from it by Langstone harbour. A quiet bathing place has been established at Hayling. Conveyances by railway to Southampton, Winchester, London, Dorchester, Chichester, Brighton, Hastings, Dover, etc. By steamers to Ryde, Cowes, Southampton, several times a day, from the Albert and Victoria piers; to Plymouth and Liverpool once a week.

SOUTHAMPTON

POPULATION, 46,960. A telegraph station. HOTELS – Radley's; The Dolphin.
ONNIBUSES to Shirley, Millbrook, Totton, and Bitterne.
STEAMERS to and from the Isle of Wight. MARKET DAYS – Tuesday,
Thursday, Friday, and Saturday. FAIRS – May 6th, Trinity Fair in Trinity week.
BANKERS – National Provincial Bank of England. Atherley & Fall; Hampshire
Banking Co.; Maddison & Pearce.

The station, which is close to the quay, and has a commanding position on the banks of the Southampton Water, is admirably adapted for the convenience of passengers. On his way to the High-street, the traveller will obtain a favourable view of the picturesque bay. Bounded on one side by the sheltering glades of the New Forest, and opening on the other to the Channel and the Isle of Wight, a series of beautiful views meet the eye, which cannot fail to charm by their exquisite contrast and variety. On leaving the terminus by the down line gate, we pass the platform, the old castle, lately the gaol, and a little further is the new Corn Market, on the site of the old Custom House, and turning to the right we enter one of the finest streets that ever ornamented a provincial town – this being High-street – a prominent object in which is the Old Bar Gate, which formed the principal entrance into the town.

Southampton is the chief mail-packet station in the kingdom, and a parliamentary borough in Hampshire (two members), seventy-nine miles from London by the South Western Railway, on a point at the head of a fine inlet called Southampton Water, into which the Test and Itchen run. Southampton has a considerable foreign and coasting trade in wine, fruit, timber, etc. When the mud banks are covered at high tide, its inlet is a fine sheet of water seven miles long, and one to two broad, and exactly the spot for a sail, with groves along the shores, especially the west, in which the nightingales are heard all night long. It is eleven or twelve miles to Cowes, opposite which is *Osborne House*, the seat of Queen Victoria.

A pleasant promenade is the Royal Victoria Pier, built in 1832. It is an elegant wooden structure, extending 246 feet into the water, having a carriage way in the centre twenty feet wide, and a footway, on each side of eight feet. A toll of twopence is required from each passenger, and the bustle that prevails on the arrival and departure of steamers causes the scene to become one of very lively interest. The Southampton Water is here three miles wide, and in the centre about forty feet in depth, so as to admit ships of any burthen. Sheltered by lofty woods, and free from all rocky obstructions, this beautiful bay presents a very convenient harbour. Bathing machines, swimming baths, and other means of salutary ablution, adapted both to the invalid and the robust, are provided for those who choose to avail themselves of the accommodation afforded. There is a regatta in July, and some well regulated races, which take place on a beautiful spot of ground on Southampton Common.

Since Southampton, owing to the advantageous effects of the railway, has become one of our leading commercial ports, some new docks have been formed, on a scale of great magnitude, and ample accommodation afforded for housing and bonding goods, as well as for the reception of shipping and the convenience of passengers passing in and out of the port. A fine excursion may be taken from Southampton to the Isle of Wight.

LYMINGTON

A telegraph station.

A town prettily situated on the right bank of the River Lymington. Its maritime operations are chiefly confined to the Isle of Wight, with which it has frequent communication. Salt is extensively manufactured in the neighbourhood. The parish church, dedicated to Thomas Becket, has many striking monuments.

CHRISTCHURCH

A telegraph station. HOTEL – King's Arms.
MARKET DAY – Monday. FAIRS – Trinity Thursday, and October 17th.

CHRISTCHURCH (at the confluence of the Avon and Stour) is a town containing some beautiful relics of the past in the ruins of its ancient collegiate church and priory, which are well worthy of notice. The church, which has been restored, is 310 feet long. It has a trade in knit and silk stockings, etc.

BOURNEMOUTH

About seven miles east of Poole, in *Hampshire*, is *Bournemouth*, a quiet bathing place in the chine of the low cliffs, among much woodland. About ten miles south-east, the Needles, rocks, and cliffs at the west end of the Isle of Wight are visible, especially in the bright gleam of a setting sun.

Below: Looking eastwards, the promenade and entrance to Bournemouth pier, *c.* 1895. *(LoC)*

Main image: A postcard photograph of the pier master of Sandown Pier on the Isle of Wight. Note the bathing machines in the background.

Inset: A Brighton Railway poster featuring the Isle, plus two seaside postcards. These early cards tended to be far more gentle in their humour and less blatantly saucy than the later variety.

BRIGHTON RAILWAY FOR ISLE OF WIGHT.

VICTORIA AND LONDON BRIDGE STATIONS FOR ISLE OF WIGHT.

SPOONING ON THE PIER.

DONT YE KNOW BETTER THAN TO LET YER CANVAS GO FLOPPING AROUND YER MAST LIKE THAT.

The Isle of Wight

This beautiful island is divided into two parts by the River Medina, or Cowes, which rises in the south, and enters the sea at the town of Cowes, opposite the mouth of Southampton Bay. The south-east coast is edged with very steep cliffs of chalk and freestone, hollowed into caverns in various parts, and vast fragments of rock are scattered along the shore. The south-west side is fenced with lofty ridges of rock, and the western extremity of them is called the Needles. Among the products are a pure white pipe clay, and a fine white crystalline sand; of the latter, great quantities are exported for the use of the glass works in various parts.

The island is accessible by way of Portsmouth, Southampton, or Lymington, from which places there are steamers to Ryde, Cowes, and Yarmouth respectively; the first two are more convenieut for Ventnor and the back of the Island; the last for Freshwater and the Needles. Supposing Ryde to be the starting point, two routes will take in almost everything in the island, which a hasty visitor would care to see. Those who desire to make a real acquaintance with all its attractions may spend many pleasant weeks in it, finding new walks every day.

RYDE

POPULATION, 3,738. Distance from station at Stokes Bay, 3 miles.
A telegraph station. HOTELS – Barnes' Royal Pier; Sivier's Hotel.
COACHES to the Eastern Route, daily. STEAMERS to and from Cowes, Portsmouth, and Southampton several times daily, from 7 a.m. to 6 p.m.
EXCURSION STEAMERS round the Island in the summer, on Mondays and Thursdays, at 12 noon fare 3s. MARKET DAYS – Tuesday and Friday.
FAIR – July 5th. REGATTA in August. MONEY ORDER OFFICE at Ryde.
BANKERS – National Provincial Bank of England, Branch Hampshire Banking Co.

RYDE is a beautiful bathing place, sloping to the sea, 25 minutes (by steam) from Portsmouth, across Spithead. Long timber pier of 2,000 ft (or two-fifths of a mile), commanding a fine prospect and a healthy blow; for which the charge is 2d per head, and ld per package! New Victoria Yacht Club House, built 1847. Chantrey's bust of Mr Sanderson, in the Market Place. Holy Trinity Church, modern Gothic, with a spire 146 feet high, Baths, hotels, lodgings (with gardens), are numerous, as are the walks and points of view around.

BRADING

Distance from station at Portsmouth, 12 miles.
Telegraph station at Ryde, 4 miles. HOTELS – Bugle; Wheat Sheaf.
COACHES to and from Newport, daily. MARKET DAY – Saturday. PAIRS – May 1st and September 21st. MONEY ORDER OFFICE at Ryde.

Ryde

Situated on the north-east coast of the Isle of Wight, Ryde is its most populous urban area. The pier, which opened in 1815, is the oldest in England, and also one of the longest with a total length of 2,234 feet.

Top left: A cluster of hotels on the esplanade in Ryde.

Middle left: Racing yachts photographed off Ryde Pier, *c.* 1910.

Below: The Needles, a row of chalk stacks on the western extremity of the island. A fourth stack, more needle-like in shape, was lost when it collapsed during a storm in 1764. *(LoC)*

BRADING, a decayed place, with an old Town Hall near the church, in which are the monuments of the Oglanders of Nunwell. In the churchyard is the grave of little Jane, the subject of one of Legh Richmond's well known stories. He was Vicar of Brading, and her cottage is pointed out under Brading Down. The harbour is like a shallow-lagoon between Bembridge Point and St Helen's old chapel. Yaverland and its curious little church, Culver Cliff, 400 feet high, with the Yarborough pillar on the top, and Whitecliff Bay below, are to the left.

SANDOWN

Distance from station at Portsmouth, 14 miles.
Telegraph station at Ventnor, 8 miles. HOTELS – Star and Garter (Hale's).
COACHES to and from Ryde and Newport, daily.
MONEY ORDER OFFICE at Shanklin.

SANDOWN, a bathing place, with a fine sweep of sandy beach, and an old fort.

SHANKLIN

Distance from the station at Portsmouth, 15 miles.
Telegraph station at Ventnor, 5 miles. HOTELS – Daish's and Williams'.
COACHES to and from Ryde and Newport, daily.
MONEY ORDER OFFICE.

This beautiful retreat is hid away among trees and corn-fields in summer, and is cleat to a chine or gash in the cliff, filled in with shrubs and trees with a good beach for walking on below. Cook's Castle, a ruined tower, 2 miles to the right. The road winds over the bold headland of Dunnose, with Shanklin Down on one side, 780 feet high, Luccombe Chine on the other. Notice the views of Sandown Bay and the country behind you. Upon descending, the first glimpse of Undercliff appears on the right, looking something like the entrance to Matlock, while the broad blue stretches away to the left.

BONCHURCH

Distance from station at Portsmouth, 20 miles.
Telegraph station at Ventnor, 2 miles. HOTEL – Bonchurch.
COACHES to and from Ryde and Newport, daily.
MONEY ORDER OFFICE at Shanklin.

BONCHURCH, so called because the church is dedicated to St Boniface. An exemplary young Clergyman, the author of *Shadows of the Cross*, and John Stirling, whose Life, written by Carlyle, has excited considerable interest, are buried in it. The road is overshadowed with trees, and passes a lake and the Pulpit Rock. There is a charming path from Shanklin to Bonchurch, through the Sandslip. Boniface Down, near Ventnor, rises steeply up 700 or 800 feet above the sea.

SANDOWN

FROM EAST

FRONT, LOOKING E.

FROM PIER HEAD

Above: Views of Sandown reproduced on a postcard, with the beach seen from the east, the front looking east, and the pier head.

Ventnor

Above: The beach and pier head seen from the east cliff, c. 1895. It was with the coming of the Isle of Wight Railway in 1866 that the town became a tourist and health resort. The pier was damaged by fire in 1985 and demolished eight years later. *Left:* An aerial photograph of Ventnor pier showing the arrangement of the landing stages for the paddle steamers.

VENTNOR

Distance from station at Portsmouth, 22 miles. A telegraph station.

HOTELS – Royal, first-class hotel and boarding establishment, of a superior description; Marine, first-class family and commercial house. Esplanade Hotel and Boarding House, situated on the beach near the sea, and close to the Baths. COACHES to and from Ryde, Cowes, and Newport.

MARKET DAY – Saturday. BANKERS – National Provincial Bank of England.

VENTNOR, the capital of Undercliff, had no existence forty years ago, but is now a respectable town, with a population of 3,208. This is owing to its delightful situation in front of the sea, and being protected by the cliff behind. Trees have not grown so fast as houses, which being of stone have a white glare in the summer sunshine; but it is in winter that its peculiar advantages are felt by the invalid, who then enjoys a climate not to be had in any other part of England except Torquay. Lodgings are abundant and moderate. Myrtles, fuchsias, and other plants grow to a large size. The Downs behind, affording endless rambles, are covered with heath and thyme. Houses occupy every accessible spot up and down the cliffs, with the Channel and the shipping perpetually in view. There is a new church, with assembly rooms, baths, etc. A fine, pebbly beach below, and attractive walks of all kinds. In the season provisions are scarce, and therefore dear, a drawback felt at Shanklin and other places on this side of the Island. Four or five coaches by way of Brading or Newport run to and fro between this and Ryde daily. Occasionally a steamer touches for Cowes or Ryde; but this is rare, and the landing is by boat. Excellent lobsters, crabs, and prawns. Some curious caves have been formed in the cliffs by the sea along the beach.

About three miles inland is *Appuldercombe*, the seat of the Earl of Yarborough, a building of the last century, in a large park on the slope of a Down, at the corner of which is the Worsley pillar. Sir R. Worsley here made a collection of marbles and paintings. Many of the family are buried in Godshill church, which is one of the best in the island, and about four miles further.

From Ventnor to Black Gang the road winds along through Undercliff, among rocks, gardens, fields, seats, farm-houses, etc., dispersed most picturesquely about in a rocky ledge or strand formed by successive landslips from the neighbouring cliff, which rises up like a wall on your right, 100 to 150 feet high, the road itself being nearly as mach above the sea, to your left. It is worth while to walk along the edge of this cliff for the sake of the panorama to be obtained of the scene below. Do not take this path at Ventnor, as it may be reached by leaving the road near St Lawrence's Well, and walking up the steps out in the face of the cliff. A footpath also winds close to the sea out of sight of the road.

CHALE

Distance from station at Portsmouth, 29 miles. Telegraph station at Ventnor, 7 miles. HOTEL – Chine. COACHES to and from Ryde and Newport, daily. MONEY ORDER OFFICE at Ventnor.

Cowes

The seaport is famous as the venue for the world's oldest regatta, Cowes Week. *Right:* Postcard view of King Edward VII being rowed to his yacht during Cowes Week. *Below:* Designed by Prince Albert, Osborne House in West Cowes was built for Queen Victoria between 1845 and 1851 as a summer retreat. She died there in January 1901.

Cowes Week: The King going on board.

Black Gang Chine is a gap in the cliff, which hangs over the beach in Chale Bay. It is bare and somewhat dark-looking, with an iron spring trickling through it. The highest point is 600 or 700 feet, making it a tiresome job to ascend or descend the steps cut in the side on a summer's day, But it is worth while to go down to the beach to watch the great waves as they roll in, especially if it is at all windy. Here the poor *Clarendon* came ashore. Behind it is *St Catherine's Down*, about 800 feet high, or 100 higher than Black Gang. There are the remains of a beacon on the top, which was used for the lighthouse till that was shifted to its present place; also a chapel or hermitage. Behind this stands a pillar, erected to commemorate the visit of a Russian Prince to this country. Though the highest point in the island, the view is by no means so good as many from the downs in the middle of it. In Chale Churchyard are the graves of several wrecked persons, especially of the crew of the *Clarendon*, East Indiaman. Hence to Freshwater is a succession of little bays and chines, none of much interest; a pathway follows the edge of the cliff. The high road passes through Thorwell (in a gap of the downs), Brixton or Bryston, and Brotlestone, all pretty places, under the downs to the right hand, which command an excellent prospect.

FRESHWATER

Distance from station at Portsmouth, 24 miles.

Telegraph station at Newport, 11 miles. HOTELS – Lanabert's Hotel; Royal Albion. COACHES to and from Hyde, Cowes, and Newport, daily.

MONEY ORDER OFFICE at Yarmouth.

FRESHWATER GATE, where the baths and lodging houses are stationed, is half a mile from the village, on the south side of the Downs, in a gap of the cliffs, which rise up 500 and 600 feet above the sea, white and dazzling, producing a grand effect. They are streaked with parallel lines of flint. Lobsters, etc., are good. Here is the residence of Alfred Tennyson, the poet laureate. Between this and the Needles are several remarkable objects, most of which can be visited only in a boat (10s, or 20s the trip), when there is little sea. Even with fine weather the long swell is apt to be disagreeable. In Freshwater Bay, fronting the baths are Deer Island; Neshanter cave, 120 feet deep, 35 wide; the Arch Rock, 600 feet out from the shore; Watcombe bay and its caves; Neptune's cave, 200 feet long; Beak cave, 90 feet; High Down Cliff, 217 feet high, swarming with puffins, razor-birds, etc.; Frenchman's Hole, 90 feet; Holmes's Parlour and Kitchen; Roe's Hell, 600 feet long, close to the Wedge Rock, so called because of a great block jammed in a gap, into which it has fallen; Old Peeper Reek; Main Bench Cliff, full of birds; Scratchell's Bay and Scratchell's Cave, 200 feet high, with an overhanging roof; Needles Cave, 300 feet long; the Needles Rocks, four or five blunt peaks, with deep water round them, at the west. end of the Island. There was a sharp rock 120 feet high, but it fell down in 1776. On the cliffs above, 469 feet high, is the lighthouse, seen 27 miles. Round this point, (or mile across the downs, from Freshwater) is...

ALUM BAY

HOTELS – Needles Hotel and boarding house.

STEAMERS to Lymington, thence per rail to Brockenhurst.

The cliffs on one side are white, and on the other are curiously variegated with strata of ochre, fuller's earth, grey and white sand, etc. Here large prawns are found. The cliffs gradually fall to Cary's Sconce, where a strong fort is being constructed. Copperas stones, lignite, or wood coal, alum, pipe clay, shells and fossils are discovered in this quarter of the Island.

YARMOUTH

Distance from station at Southampton, 19 miles.

Telegraph station at Newport, 10 miles. HOTEL – George.

CARRIERS to and from Cowes, Newport, and all parts of the Island, daily.

STEAMERS to Lymington and Cowes, daily. Fares, Lymington, 1s 6d and 1s; Day Tickets, 3s. To Cowes, 2s 6d and 1s 6d; Day Tickets, 4s and 2s 6d.

MARKET DAY – Friday. FAIR – July 25th.

YARMOUTH, another decayed borough, originally founded by the Rivers family. There is a town hall, one of Henry VIII's forts, and a church, in which is a monument of Sir Robert Holmes, Captain of the Island, at the visit of Charles II in 1671. He resided at what is now the King's Head Inn. Hurst Castle is opposite.

WEST COWES

POPULATION, 5,422. Distance from station at Southampton, 11 miles.

A telegraph station. HOTEL – Fountain. COACHES to and from Ryde and Newport, daily. VESSELS – The rendezvous of ships of all nations for orders.

STEAM VESSELS to Portsmouth, Ryde, and Southampton, six times a day; to Yarmouth, once daily. REGATTA in August.

MONEY ORDER OFFICE. BANKERS – National Provincial Bank of England.

COWES, five miles from Newport. An immense quantity of shipping call off here annually, from all parts of the globe, for orders from their owners or consignees, as to the destination of their cargoes; and in the winter months fleets of merchantmen of all nations rendezvous here weatherbound. It lies at the mouth the Medina and is a stirring port, noted for its shipbuilding (especially at White's yard), and yachting. There is deep water here; the Royal Yacht Club hold their regatta in August. Handsome Clubhouse, Old castle, built by Henry VIII, from which Cowes derives its name. Dr Arnold was a native of Cowes. There is a ferry to East Cowes, across the Medina, beyond which *Norris Castle* and *Osborne House* are visible. Sailing boats 2s per hour.

On the beach are bathing machines, and it is much visited by fashionable company.

Dorsetshire

Which is bounded on the north by Wiltshire, on the east by Hampshire, on the west by Devon and part of Somerset, and on the south by the British Channel. Its form is everywhere irregular; its long northern side has a considerable angular projection in the middle; the sea shore on the south runs out into numerous points and headlands, till it stretches to the Isle of Portland; thence westward the coast is not so deeply indented, but inclines obliquely toward Devonshire.

POOLE

Distance from station, 2 miles. A telegraph station. HOTEL – Antelope.
OMNIBUSES to and from Parkstone and Bournemouth.
MARKET DAYS – Monday and Thursday. FAIRS – May 1st, and November 2nd.

A Dorsetshire borough and port, on the South Western Railway, 122 miles from London, by a small branch out of the main line. The neighbourhood is a dreary plain. of sand and furze. Population 9,759, who return two members. Having been founded since the Conquest, it is a comparatively modern town, but has always preserved a respectable position as a third or fourth class port. The harbour, though six or seven miles long, and nearly as broad (when the tide is up), is choked with sand, but there is a good deep-water channel inside the bar. Salt fish and American timber are imported; and one of the chief exports is potters' clay from Purbeck, of so good a quality that it is proposed to establish potteries on a great scale here – especially as the transit for coal is now easy and direct. There are two miles of quay room. Here Charles X landed 1830, after his flight from Paris.

The town is pretty well built, on a point of land between the harbour and Holes Bay, (the entrance to which is crossed by a bridge at the bottom of High Street), but offers nothing remarkable in its public structures, except an old disused town hall built 1572, and the large modern church, in which is an altar-piece of carved work. One piece of antiquity is an old gate built in the reign of Richard III. In the middle of the harbour (or pool, which gives name to the town), is *Brownsea Island*, the seat of Sir S. Foster, Bart. Near the mouth of the harbour is an oyster bank, from which vast quantities are carried to the creeks of Essex and the Thames.

WEYMOUTH

A telegraph station. HOTELS – Luces's Royal; Drew's Victoria; Jeffries.
MARKET DAYS – Tuesday and Friday. RACES – in September.
BANKERS – Eliot & Pearce.

Nothing can be more striking and picturesque than the situation of this delightful watering-place. The town is built on the western shore of one of the finest bays in

Poole

Left: Postcard image of the quay at Poole.

Below: Chesil Beach, an 18-mile-long beach of shingle to the west of Weymouth. It derives its name from *cisel*, meaning gravel.

Weymouth

Below left: Two views of Weymouth harbour and a busy Esplanade. The curved beach was frequented by King George III during his illness. *Below:* A rare wartime colour photo of the intensive activity at Weymouth immediately before the D-Day landings in June 1944. The harbour was an important embarkation point for many vessels, some protected from low-flying aircraft by these shipborne barrage balloons. *(NARA)*

the English Channel, and being separated into two parts by the river, which forms a commodious harbour, it is most conveniently situated for trade. Population, 11,383. A long and handsome bridge of two arches, constructed of stone, with a swivel in the centre, was erected in 1820, and thus the divided townships enjoy a communication. The town, especially on the Melcombe side of the harbour, is regularly built, and consists chiefly of two principal streets, parallel with each other, intersected with others at right angles; it is well paved and lighted, and is tolerably supplied with fresh water. Since the town has become a place of fashionable resort for sea-bathing, various handsome ranges of buildings, and a theatre, assembly rooms, and other places of fashionable entertainment, have been erected, and these are now rapidly extending and increasing in every direction. The principal of these are Belvidere, the Crescent, Gloucester Row, Royal Terrace, Chesterfield Place, York Buildings, Charlotte Row, Augusta Place; and Clarence, Pulteney, and Devonshire Buildings, are conspicuous; to which may perhaps be added Brunswick Buildings, a handsome range of houses at the entrance of the town. From the windows of these buildings, which front the sea, a most extensive and delightful view is obtained, comprehending on the left a noble range of hills and cliffs, extending for many miles in a direction from west to east, and of the sea in front, with the numerous vessels, yachts, and pleasure boats, which are continually entering and leaving the harbour.

To the west of the harbour are the barracks, a very neat and commodious range of buildings. The Esplanade is one of the finest marine promenades in the kingdom. It is a beautiful terrace, thirty feet broad, rising from the sands, and secured by a strong wall, extending in a circular direction parallel with the bay for nearly a mile, and commanding a most beautiful panorama of the sea, cliffs, and the mountainous range of rocks by which the bay is enclosed.

On the Esplanade is the Royal Lodge where George III and the Royal family resided, and here also will be found the principal public libraries, vetoing with the dulcet strains of some experimental musician.

The Theatre is a neat, and well arranged edifice in Augusta Place, but it is seldom inconveniently crowded. Races are held early in September, and during their continuance a splendid regatta is celebrated in the bay, which has a fine circular sweep of two miles; and being sheltered by a contiguous range of hills from the north and northeast winds, the water is generally very calm and transparent. The sands are smooth, firm, and level, and so gradual is the descent towards the sea, that, at the distance of 100 yards, the water is not more than two feet deep. Bathing-machines of the usual number and variety are in constant attendance, and on the South Parade is an establishment of hot salt-water baths, furnished with dressing-rooms and every requisite accommodation. At the south entrance of the harbour are the higher and lower jetties, the latter of which is a little to the east of the former. The sea has been for a long series of years retiring from the eastern side of the harbour, and part of the ground over which it formerly flowed is now covered with buildings, other parts being enclosed with iron railings, which form a prominent feature on the Esplanade. On the Weymouth side are the Look Out and the Nothe, affording extensive and interesting prospects; on the latter is a battery, formerly mounted with six pieces of ordnance, which, on the fort being dismantled, were removed into Portland Castle. Within the walls a signal post bas been established, which communicates with several other stations, and apartments have been built for the accommodation of a lieutenant and a party of men. The bay affords ample facilities for aquatic excursions at any time, its tranquil surface being never disturbed except by violent storms from the south or south-west. Yachts and pleasure boats are always in readiness, and the fares kept strictly under municipal supervision.

No place can be more salubrious than Weymouth. The air is so pure and mild, that the Lowe is not only frequented during the summer, but has been selected by many opulent families as a permanent residence; and the advantage which it possesses in the excellence of its bay, the beauty of its scenery, and the healthfulness of its climate, have contributed to raise it from the low state into which it had fallen from the depression of its commerce, to one of the most flourishing towns in the kingdom.

About a mile to the south-west are the remains of Weymouth or Sandsfoot Castle, erected by Henry VIII in the year 1539, and described by Leyland as 'a right goodly and warlyke castle, having one open barbicane.' The burning cliff at Weymouth – a kind of miniature volcano – has long attracted the notice of naturalists, and will well repay a visit. At Nottington, about two miles and a-half distant, on the Dorchester road, is a mineral spring, the water of which is considered efficacious in cases of scrofula.

About four miles south from Weymouth, is the island of Portland, which, though thus called, is in reality, a peninsula, connected with the mainland by an extremely narrow isthmus, called Chesil Bank, a line of shingles thrown up by the sea, and extending for more than eight miles, from Portland to Abbotsbury, It is not more than two miles broad and four long; and though the shores are steep and rugged, the surface of the soil at the summit is smooth, and yields wheat, oats, and barley of average quality. At the southern extremity, called Portland Bill, are the higher and lower lighthouses, and a signal station, called the 'Lewes'; near the former is a remarkable cavern, from which the water rises as from a fountain. On the eastern side are Rufus and Pennsylvania Castles, and on the northern side are Portland Castle, and another signal station.

A trip to the Island is one of the most favourite excursions generally offered, among other temptations, to travellers, and will furnish materials for an interesting day's enjoyment. Indeed, this picturesque coast is unrivalled. The sea view is agreeably diversified with grand and striking objects, to break the monotony that usually pervades a marine prospect. The coast of this part of Dorsetshire itself presents also grand and striking points. St Alban's Head and Lulworth Cove, with their bold and soaring cliffs, are sublime and astonishing features in the vast picture that we look upon from hence. The surrounding country is full of castellated remains and interesting historical associations. In the neighbouring isle of Purbeck are the ruins of Corfe Castle, memorable for the assassination of King Edward the Martyr.

Milton Abbey is even yet beautiful, under the decaying winters of many ages; and at Sherborne Castle there are many architectural fragments that still attest the genius of the ill-fated but high-minded Raleigh, and a garden, too, whose shades, planted by his hand, now overlook and wave above those walls which once afforded them shelter, honour, and protection. The rides about Smallmouth Sands, Upway, and beyond the source of the River Wey, are replete with picturesque and ever-changing objects, and the beauty of the town itself is not a little enhanced by the remaining ruins of Weymouth Castle, a scanty relic of the troublous times of old.

The latitude of Weymouth is one degree farther south than London, and many plants which require protection from the cold in other parts of the country here flourish through the winter in the open air. The geranium grows luxuriantly, and requires little care, and the large and small-leaved myrtle are out-of-door plants. Indeed, so salubrious is the climate that Dr Arbuthnot, who came in his early days to settle at Weymouth, observed that no physician could either live or die there. This, however, savours more of flattery than fact, as present observation will fully testify.

As a place for sea-bathing Weymouth is perfect, and the accommodation of about twenty or thirty machines, always ready, near the centre of the Esplanade, greatly facilitates that operation. The sands over which the bathers have to walk are well known as of the finest description; the declivity of the shore is almost imperceptible, and totally free from those obstructions which are noticed on many parts of the southern coast, so that the most timid can indulge in the luxury of open sea-bathing, with the additional comfort of perfect security and of sea-water, pure, clean and transparent. Neat and commodious warm salt-water baths will also be found on the South Parade, opposite the harbour.

Abbotsbury, near the west end of the fleet or lake inside the Chesil Bank, is the seat of the Earl of Ilchester, and has a decoy and swannery.

BRIDPORT
A telegraph station. HOTEL – Bull.

A small port on the river Brit, noted from the earliest period for its hempen manufactures. Its staple productions are twine, fishing nets, and canvas, and much hemp for the purpose is grown. 'He was stabbed with a Bridport dagger' was an old saying for a man that was hung.

The South Devon Railway

This line was to have a troubled existence. Isambard Kingdom Brunel had persuaded the directors that the atmospheric method of propulsion was the way to go for the section between Exeter, above, and Totnes. It failed when rats gnawed the leather flaps sealing the pipes, and they reverted to conventional locomotives instead. The line itself followed the coast for much of the route and landslips and storm damage were a regular feature, as shown below in this engraving of a fall near Dawlish in 1852. The sea wall at Dawlish made the headlines again when it was breached in the winter storms of 2014. *(LoC)*

South Devon

This county is one of the most beautiful in England, and in point of size is only exceeded by that of York. It is about 280 miles in circuit. Its external appearance is varied and irregular; and the heights in many parts, particularly in the vicinity of Dartmouth, swell into mountains. Dartmoor, and the waste called Dartmoor Forest, occupy the greater portion of the western district, which extends from the vale of Exeter to the banks of the river Tamar.

EXMOUTH

A telegraph station.

This place has, within the last few years, made rapid strides in the march of improvement. The Beacon Hill is covered with buildings, and the Parade is stretching away right and left, with no visible signs, hitherto, of limitation.

Situated on the eastern side of the River Exe, two projecting sand banks form a partial enclosure, leaving an opening of about one-third the width of the harbour. The Exe is here about a mile and a half across, and though the entrance is somewhat difficult, the harbour is very convenient, and will admit the passage of ships of more than 300 tons burden.

There are two good inns, numerous boarding-houses and apartments, and a good subscription library and reading-room, but the visitor must create his own amusement, chiefly in the rides or pedestrian excursions, which the beauty of the surrounding country will so well afford the opportunity of enjoying. The proper time for bathing here is at high water, but there are hot and cold baths that can be taken at any hour, conveniently situated under the Beacon Terrace. Like many other maritime towns in Devonshire, Exmouth has in its immediate neighbourhood a valley sheltered on all sides from the winds, and capable of affording a genial retreat to those affected with complaints in the lungs. This will be found at Salterton, four miles to the east, and here the romantic caverns of the secluded bay, the rough but richly-pebbled beach, and the continuous marine prospect, will form irresistible temptations to explore the way thither. Dr Clarke says, in speaking of the climate:

> Exmouth is decidedly a healthy place, and notwithstanding the whole of this coast is rather humid, agues are almost unknown.

Invalids often experience the greatest benefit from a residence here, more particularly on the Beacon Hill, the most elevated and finest situation in the neighbourhood, and which, as some compensation for the south-west gales, commands one of the most magnificent views in Devonshire. Along the southern base of this hill there is also a road of considerable extent, protected from the north and north-east winds, and well suited for exercise when they prevail; and here it may be remarked, that between the summer climate of North and South Devon there is as marked a difference as between the cast of their scenery, the air of the former being keen and bracing, and its features romantic and picturesque, while in the latter the rich softness of the landscape harmonizes with the soft and soothing qualities of the climate. An omnibus runs twice a-week from Exmouth to Sidmouth.

About a mile from Exmouth is the secluded and picturesque village of Withycombe, and two miles further a fine old ruin, known as the Church of St John in the Wilderness, will attract attention. It was built probably in the reign of Henry VII, but the old tower, one of the aisles, and part of the pulpit, now alone remain.

Sidmouth, eleven miles from Exmouth, is one of the most agreeably-situated little watering-places that can be imagined. It lies nestled in the bottom of a valley, opening to the sea between two lofty hills, 500 feet high, whence a most extensive and varied prospect of a beautiful part of the country is afforded on one side; and on the other a view of the open sea, bounded by a line of coast which stretches from Portland Isle, on the east, to Torbay, on the west. The summit of Peak Hill, on the west, is a lofty ridge, extending from north to south; that of Salcombe Hill, on the east, is much broader, and affords room for a race-course: both are highest towards the sea, where they terminate abruptly, forming a precipice of great depth, on the very verge of which the labourer may be seen guiding the plough several hundred feet perpendicular above the sea.

Although Sidmouth is irregularly built, its appearance is generally neat, occasionally highly picturesque, and in some parts positively handsome. The magnificent villas and cottages on the slopes are, almost without exception, surrounded with gardens; they command pleasing prospects, and are delightfully accessible by shady lanes, which wind up the hills, and intersect each other in all directions. Old local topographers speak of Sidmouth as a considerable fishing town, and as carrying on some trade with Newfoundland, but its harbour is now

Above: The distinctive red cliffs of south Devon; these are at Sidmouth. *(Touriste)*

totally choked up with rocks, which at low water are seen covered with sea-weed, stretching away to a considerable distance from the shore. Its history may be very briefly recounted. The manor of Sidmouth was presented by William the Conqueror to the Abbey of St Michel in Normandy, and was afterwards taken session of by the Crown, during the wars with France, as the property of an alien foundation. It was afterwards granted to the monastery of Sion, with which it remained until the dissolution.

Hotels, boarding and lodging-houses are scattered over every part of Sidmouth and its vicinity, and the local arrangements are throughout excellent. The public buildings are soon enumerated, for they only consist of a church, near the centre of the town, a very ordinary edifice of the fifteenth century, enlarged from time to time, a neat little chapel of ease, and a new market-house, built in 1840. Around here, and in the Fore-street, are some excellent shops, and the town is well supplied with gas and water. The sea-wall was completed in 1838. There was formerly an extensive bank of sand and gravel, thrown up by the sea, a considerable distance from the front of the town, but this being washed away in a tremendous storm, this defence was resorted to as a more permanent protection from the encroachment of the waves. It now forms an agreeable promenade, upwards of 1,700 feet long.

Sidmouth is sheltered by its hills from every quarter, except the south, where it is open to the sea, and has an atmosphere strongly impregnated with saline particles. Snow is very rarely witnessed, and in extremely severe seasons, when the surrounding hills are deeply covered, not a vestige, not a flake, will remain in this warm and secluded vale. The average mean winter temperature is from four to five degrees warmer than London, and eight degrees warmer than the northern watering-places.

'In Sidmouth and its neighbourhood' (says the author of *The Route Book of Devon*), 'will be found an inexhaustible mine for the study and amusement of the botanist, geologist, or conchologist. A very curious relic of antiquity was found on the beach here about five years since – a Roman bronze standard or centaur, representing the centaur Chiron, with his pupil Achilles behind his back. The bronze is cast hollow, and is about nine inches in height. The left fore leg of the centaur is broken, and the right hind leg mutilated. The under part or pedestal formed a socket, by which the standard was screwed on a pole or staff.'

The present great features of interest in the neighbourhood are the landslips, ten miles distant, which, extending along the coast from Sidmouth to Lyme Regis, are most interesting to the geologist and the lover of nature. This range of cliffs, extending from Haven to Pinhay, has been the theatre of two convulsions, or landslips, one commencing on Christmas-day, 1839, at Bendon and Dowlands, whereby forty-five acres of arable land were lost to cultivation – the other about five weeks after, on the 3rd of February, 1840, at Whitlands, little more than a mile to the eastward of the former, but much smaller in magnitude than the previous one.

There are one or two situations, says an excellent local authority, overlooking the western or great landslip, which seems to be admired as peculiarly striking – the view of the great chasm, looking east-ward, and the view from Dowlands,

Left: At Dawlish the railway separates the town from the sea front. The footbridge over the line can be seen in the background.

Main image: A curve in the sea wall to the north-east of Teignmouth, with the Parson and Clerk Rocks visible in the distance. The outer stack, the Clerk, lost his head in a storm in 2003.

looking west-ward, upon the undercliff and new beach. The best prospect, perhaps, for seeing the extraordinary nature of the whole district, combined with scenery, is from Pinhay and Whitlands, and looking inland you see the precipitous yet wooded summit of the main land, and the castellated crags of tile ivy-clad rocks, on the terraces immediately below, and the deep dingle which separates you from it. By turning a little to the north-east, Pinhay presents itself chalky pinnacles and descending terraces; whilst to the west the double range and high perpendicular cliffs of Rowesdown offer themselves. By turning towards the sea is embraced the whole range of the great bay of Dorset and Devon, extending from Portland on the east to Start Point on the west, bounded on either side by scenery of the finest coast character.

Exeter to Torquay and Plymouth

This part of the line is invested with additional interest, from the magnificent scenery that opens on each side as we proceed. There is scarcely a mile traversed which does not unfold some peculiar picturesque charm or new feature of its own to make the eye 'dazzled and drunk with beauty'.

Once at Exeter, we have all the romantic allurements of the watering places of the west within our reach, where the possessor of robust health may find a fund of illimitable enjoyment in the rich bouquet that nature has spread before him on the freshening shores of Devon, and the invalid, those desired qualifications most conducive to a speedy and permanent convalescence.

On leaving Exeter we pass in rapid succession the stations of ST THOMAS, EXMINSTER, and STAR CROSS, and in a very few minutes arrive at...

DAWLISH

POPULATION, 3,505. A telegraph station. HOTELS – London; Royal.

DAWLISH, one of the stations of the South Devon Railway, is one of the prettiest places along the coast to pass a quiet summer month. Within the last century, rising from a mere fishing village to the dignity of a fashionable watering-place, it has become extended from the valley in which it lies to a considerable distance east and west; and though the incursion of the railroad has materially affected the fine expanse of the esplanade, it still possesses an excellent beach, bounded on the east by the Langstone Cliffs, and on the west by the rocks familiarly known by the appellation of the Parson and Clerk. The bathing is exceedingly good, and the facilities afforded for its enjoyment admirably arranged. The houses, built in handsome terraces along the sides of the hill and strand, and fronted by lawns and gardens, are very handsome and picturesque, the majority of them commanding an ample sea view. The parish church is at the upper end of the town, and was partly rebuilt in 1824, being rendered sufficiently commodious to accommodate a congregation of nearly two thousand people. There is a good organ, and a handsome window of stained glass in the interior.

Torquay

Three colour postcards for Torquay in Tor Bay. The settlements of Torquay, Paignton and Brixham are known collectively as Torbay. According to Bradshaw, Torquay has been described as 'the Montpelier of England'.

Above: Advertising card for the Rosetor and Erin Hall private hotels.

Left: Another advertising card, this time for the Hotel Regina, *c.* 1930.

Bottom left: The Princess Gardens Jetty at Torquay.

The walks and drives in the vicinity of the town are remarkably pretty and interesting, the shady lanes at the back, winding through the declivity of the hills, affording an endless variety of inland and marine scenery. The climate is considered more genial even than that of Torquay; but so nearly do these places approximate that, for all general purposes, the remarks made upon the atmospherical characteristics of Torquay will be found equally applicable to those of Dawlish. Of late years, considerable improvement has been of in the watching and lighting arrangements of the town, and some new buildings have added much to its external beauty. A new church in the Gothic style, St Mark's, has recently been erected. Circulating libraries and hotels, with the other usual accessories to a fashionable marine resort, are numerous and well provided, and the excursionist may here crown the enjoyments of the day with such a stroll on the beach by moonlight as can be obtained at few other places. One of the most delightful excursions in the neighbourhood is to *Luscombe Park*, the seat of Hoare, Esq. Good facilities for boating and fishing by applying to Coombe, a trustworthy old seaman.

TEIGNMOUTH

POPULATION, 6,922. A telegraph station. HOTELS – Royal; Devon.

TEIGNMOUTH, three miles from Dawlish, is recognised as the largest watering-place on the Devonian coast; but, from the irregularity of the streets, it is only in the esplanade that it can rival the others before named. A large export trade is carried on here, which gives a life and animation to the streets, and the bustle that occasionally prevails is often felt as an agreeable change to the monotony of a country residence. The air is more bracing and considerably colder than at Dawlish or Torquay, the town being much exposed to the east winds. In respect both to the excellence and accommodation of houses and apartments, there are few places more convenient for either a temporary or permanent residence than Teignmouth. An excellent supply of gas and water is enjoyed by the town, and all the comforts, with most of the luxuries, of life are easily and economically obtainable. There are two churches, situated respectively in East and West Teignmouth, the former being the more modern, and the latter – particularly as regards the interior – being the more interesting. The Assembly Rooms, with Subscription, Reading, Billiard, and News Rooms attached, furnish an agreeable source of amusement, and libraries are, with hotels, plentifully scattered through the town.

The river Teign, which here flows into the Channel, yields an abundant supply of fish, and the pleasure of a sail up the river to the interior is to be numbered among the allurements of a sojourn. A bridge, considered the longest in England, has been thrown across the Teign at this point, erected in 1827, at a cost of nearly £20,000. It is 1,672 feet in length, and consists of thirty-four arches, with a drawbridge over the deepest part of the channel, to allow free passage for vessels.

Near the mouth of the river is a lighthouse exhibiting a red light. The noble esplanade – or Teignmouth Den, as it is curiously styled – is a deservedly favourite promenade with all visitors, and the bold and towering cliffs that overhang the sea impart a most romantic aspect to the surrounding scenery. Excursions either on sea or land may be made from Teignmouth with the greatest of facility of conveyance, and the environs are so extremely rich in natural and artificial attractions that they are almost inexhaustible. Three fairs are held in the months of January, February, and September, and an annual regatta takes place in August. The post-office is in Bank Street.

TORQUAY

POPULATION, 16,419. Distance from station, 1¼ mile.

A telegraph station. HOTELS – Royal; Apsley House.

TORQUAY has been somewhat characteristically described as the Montpelier of England, and truly it is deserving of the appellation. Situated in a small bay at the north-eastern corner of Torbay, the larger one, it is sheltered by a ridge of hills clothed by verdant woodland to the summit, and has thus an immunity from the cold northern and easterly winds, which few other spots so completely enjoy. From being a small village with a few scattered houses, chiefly occupied by officers' wives, during the period of the last French war, when the Channel fleet were at anchor opposite, it has rapidly risen to a thriving populous town. To borrow the description of *The Route Book of Devon*:

> The town beginning with the lower tier, is built round the three sides of the strand or quay formed by the pier, and is composed chiefly of shops of the tradesmen, having a row of trees in front, planted between the flag pavement and the carriage way. The next tier, which is approached by a winding road at each end, and steps at other places, is comprised of handsome terraces; and the third, or highest, having a range of beautiful villas. The views from either of these levels are most enchanting, taking in the whole of the fine expansive roadstead of Torbay, within whose circumference numerous fleets can ride in safety, and where is always to be seen the trim yacht and pleasure-boat, the dusky sail of the Brixham trawler, or coasting merchantman, and frequently the more proud and spirit-stirring leviathan of the deep – one of Britain's best bulwarks – a man-of-war. To this also must be added, the beautiful country surrounding, commencing by Berry Head to the south, until your eye rests upon the opposite extremity, encircling within its scope the town of Brixham, the richly cultivated neighbourhood of Godrington and Paignton, with the picturesque church of the latter, and the sands rounding from it to the fine woods of Tor Abbey, and the town and pier immediately below. But it is not within the circle of the town of Torquay, such as we have described, that residences for strangers and invalids are exclusively to be found; the sides and summits of the beautiful valleys which open from it are dotted over with cottages, pavilions, and detached villas, to the extent of two or three miles, in every direction, to which the different roads diverge. About half a mile from Torquay, in the once secluded cove of Meadfoot,

which is now being converted into a second town, terraces surpassing those in Torquay are already rising, and the forest of villas has connected the two towns. The sea views from these heights are magnificent, and the situation most attractive.

This, though it must be admitted a very alluring picture, falls far short of the reality, as bursts upon the eye of the stranger who visits it for the first time. The groupings of the various villas and the picturesque vistas which every turning in the road discloses, are enough to throw a painter into ecstacies, and render his portfolio plethoric with sketches. As before stated, the whole of the buildings are of modern origin. The pier, which forms a most agreeable promenade, was begun in 1804 and with the eastern pier, about forty feet wide, encloses a basin of some 300 feet long by 500 broad. This is the favourite lounge. Another on the Torwood-road is the 'Public Gardens', skillfully laid out under the direction of the lord of the manor, who has placed about four acres of his estate at the disposal of the public.

Passing up the new road, made under Walton Hill, to the Paignton Sands, we come to the remains of Tor Abbey, once more richly endowed than any in England; and now forming a portion of the delightful seat belonging to Mrs Cray, a munificent patroness of the town. Between Torquay and Babbicombe is Kent's Cavern, or Hole, consisting of a large natural excavation capable of being explored to the extent of 600 feet from the entrance. Dr Buckland here discovered numerous bones of bears, hyenas, elephants, and other expatriated animals, now no longer happily found in this country. Amusements of every kind are easily attainable. A theatre, concerts – held at Webb's Royal Hotel – assemblies, libraries, news and billiard rooms, catering for every imaginable taste, and the Torquay Museum, belonging to the Natural History Society there, has a most valuable collection. An excellent market, inns proportionate to the depths of every purse, and apartments to be obtained at reasonable rates, form not the least of the advantages to be derived from a protracted sojourn in this delightful region; but there is one greater attraction yet – its climate.

If those English invalids who, in search of a more congenial temperature, hastily enter on a long journey to some foreign country, and wilfully encounter all the inconveniences attending a residence there, were but to make themselves acquainted with the bland and beautiful climates which lie within an easy jaunt, and offer their own accustomed comforts in addition, how many a fruitless regret and unavailing repentance might hereafter be spared. To all suffering under pulmonary complaints, Torquay offers the greatest inducement for a trial of its efficacy as a place of winter residence. Dr James Clark, in his excellent work on climate, says:

The general character of the climate of this coast is soft and humid. Torquay is certainly drier than the other places, and almost entirely free from fogs. This drier state of the atmosphere probably arises in part from the limestone rocks, which are confined to the neighbourhood of this place, and partly from its position between the two streams, the Dart and the Teign, by which the rain is in

Teignmouth
Above: Looking west across the railway cutting where the railway sea wall turns inland. The South Devon Railway's station for Teignmouth had opened on 30 May 1846. *(LoC)*

Brixham
Below: The harbour in Brixham. As the Bradshaw guide noted in 1863, the town was chiefly noted for its extensive fisheries, 'employing more than two hundred vessels'. *(LoC)*

some degree attracted. Torquay is also remarkably protected from the north-east winds, the great evil of our spring climate; it is likewise well sheltered from the north-west. This protection from winds extends over a very considerable tract of beautiful country, abounding in every variety of landscape, so that there is scarcely a wind that blows from which the invalid will not be able to find a shelter for exercise either on foot or horseback. In this respect Torquay is most superior to any other place we have noticed. It possesses all the advantages of the south-western climate in the highest degree, and, with the exception of its exposure to the south-west gales, partakes less of the disadvantages of it than any other place having accommodation for invalids. The selection will, I believe, lie among the following places as winter and spring residences – Torquay, Undercliff, Hastings, and Clifton; and perhaps, in the generality of cases, will deserve the preference in the order stated.

So high an eulogium from so impartial and eminent an authority has seldom been bestowed. That it is well deserved, however, may be further seen from the meteorological observations registered, which give the mean winter temperature as about 46 degrees, being five degrees warmer than even Exeter. In summer, from the cooling influence of the sea breeze, the temperature, during the last five years, has never at the highest exceeded 80 degrees. So equable a temperature is, we believe, not to be met with elsewhere in Great Britain.

A delightful sandy beach, within ten minutes' walk of the town, presents facilities for sea-bathing that render a plunge into the clear and sparkling bosom of the bay perfectly irresistible to all who have the taste for its enjoyment. Bathing machines and baths of every description may be had between Torquay and its suburb Paignton, and as a brisk walk after so refreshing a submersion is the orthodox sequel, it may be some satisfaction for the pedestrian to know that the environs abound in those landscape-looking vistas seen through green lanes and over-arching woodland which form the true characteristic of Devonian scenery.

PAIGNTON STATION. The situation of this place is really beautiful, commanding a central aspect of Torbay. Its picturesque church and the sands rounding from it to the line woods of Tor Abbey, and the town and pier below it, form a pleasing coup d'oeil.

BRIXHAM ROAD station.

BRIXHAM

Close at hand, is chiefly noted for its extensive fisheries, employing more than two hundred vessels and fifteen hundred seamen. The weekly average amount received for fish is no less than £600. It was here that the Prince of Orange landed, and to commemorate the event a monument has been fixed in the centre of the fish-market, with a portion of the identical stone he first stepped upon inserted, and inscribed thus: 'On this stone, and near this spot, William Prince of Orange first set foot, on his landing in England, 4th of November, 1688.'

Early Victorian Humour.

"OLD 'UN, LET'S HAVE A 'POUND' OF OYSTERS."
"WE SELLS 'EM BY 'MEASURE,' SIR."
"DO YER? OH WELL, THEN, LET'S HAVE A 'YARD.'"

Plymouth

Although primarily a naval dockyard, Plymouth was an important stopping point on the Great Western Railway and the base for 'endless excursions'.

Above: Brunel's tubular railway bridge across the Tamar, as depicted by the artist Terence Cuneo.

Left: An interesting postcard showing an example of 'Early Victorian Humour'.

Below: Plymouth's pier on the Hoe, opened in May 1884, demolished in 1953.

The railway being yet incomplete, omnibuses run in connection with the trains from Brixham Road and with the ferry across the River Dart to...

DARTMOUTH

A telegraph station. HOTELS – Commercial; Castle.

This sea-port town is situated at the mouth or the River Dart, navigable about ten miles inland. Population, 4,444. Its harbour is very capacious, affording safe anchorage for five hundred large vessels at the same time. The coast scenery here is exceedingly romantic, and the excursion hence made to the source of the Dart is one of the great attractions with visitors.

PLYMOUTH

A telegraph station. HOTELS – Royal Hotel; Chubbs' Commercial.
FLY CHARGES – For two persons, any distance, not exceeding one mile 8*d*; every additional half-mile, 4*d*. For three or four persons per mile, or fraction of a mile, 1*s*; every additional half-mile, 6*d*. No fare, however, to be leas than 1*s*.
BANKERS – Branch of the Bank of England; Harris & Co.; Devon & Cornwall Banking Co.

A borough, first class fortress, and naval dockyard in Devonshire, at the mouth of the Channel, 246 miles from London by the Great Western Railway. The dockyard and harbour are at Devonport, the victualling office is at Stonehouse, and there are other establishments in the neighbourhood, but Plymouth is the common name for all.

EXCURSIONS FROM PLYMOUTH. These are almost endless in variety, and equally beautiful. The visitor will be soon made acquainted with clotted cream, junket, white pot, squab pie, and other west country mysteries and the unbounded hospitality of the people. Within a few miles are the following: *Mount-Edgecumbe* (on the Cornwall side of the Sound), the seat of Earl Mount-Edgecumbe, in a beautiful park, overlooking Plymouth, the breakwater, sea, etc. A fort in the Sound was first built when the Armada invaded these shores; and it was from this port that Howard of Effingham, Drake, and Hawkins, sailed out to attack it. *Deus afflavit, et dissipantur*; and where is Spain now!

Almost before we get clear of Plymouth arrival is announced at...

DEVONPORT

A telegraph station.

A place of great importance, partly overlooking the Sound (where it is defended by Mount Wise battery), and the anchorage at the Tamar's mouth, called Hamaoze. Here is the royal Dockyard, on a space of 71 acres, inclusive of five more at the Gun Wharf (built by Sir J. Vanburgh). The Dockyard includes various docks and building slips, storehouses, a rope house 200 fathoms long, blacksmiths' shop, etc.

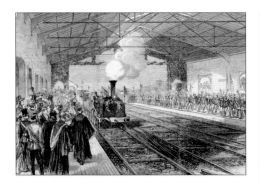

CORNWALL

The Cornish Riviera
The term was coined by the GWR's publicity department and the company's posters and brochures, shown left and above, conjure images of semi-Mediterranean climes.

Falmouth
Top left: The extension to Famouth was built by the Cornwall Railway and opened on 24 August 1864, the year after Bradshaw's guide was published. This is the scene as the first broad gauge train arrived at the station. *Below:* A twentieth-century postcard of the harbour.

The CORNISH RIVIERA

The Harbour, Falmouth

Cornwall

CORNWALL, from its soil, appearance, and climate, is one of the least inviting of the Eaglish counties. A ridge of bare and rugged hills, inter-mixed with bleak moors, runs through the midst of its whole length, and exhibits the appearance of a dreary waste. The most important objects in the history of this county are its numerous mines, which for centuries have furnished employment to thousands of its inhabitants; and the trade to which they give birth, when considered in a national point of view, is of the greatest relative consequence. In a narrow slip of land, where the purposes of agriculture would not employ above a few thousand inhabitants, the mines alone support a population estimated at more than 80,000 labourers, exclusive of artisans. The principle produce of the Cornish mines is tin, copper, and lead. The strata in which these metals are found extend from the Land's End, in a direction from west to east, entirely along the country into Devonshire. Nearly all the metals are found in veins or fissures, the direction of which is generally east and west. The annual value of the copper mines has been estimated at £350,000. Logan stones deserve to be mentioned amongst the curiosities of this county. They are of great weight, and poised on the top of immense piles of rocks.

Falmouth was formerly an important mail packet station. Below it are Pendennis Castle and St Anthony's Light, on the opposite sides of the entrance. The former, built by Henry VIII, was famous in the civil war for its resistance to parliament, against whose forces it held out till 1646. The richest mines are in the granite moorlands to the north, near St Agnes, etc., or in the neighbourhood of the rail to Penzance. At Perranzabulae, 5 miles from Truro, an ancient British church was uncovered, 25 feet in 1835, by shifting sands (which in former times overwhelmed everything on this side of the coast), and gave occasion to Mr Trelawney's work, the *Lost Church Found*, in which he shows what the primitive English church was before corrupted by Popery. This and other parishes were named from the famous St Tiran, the patron of tinners, who, like many other eminent preachers of that age, came from Ireland. The story is that he sailed over on a mill stone, but perhaps this was the name of the ship. Near St Agnes Beacon is a camp called Picran Round, Chacewater, Wheal Towan, Wheal Leisure, Pen Hale, Perran St George (all near Perran Porth, the last 100 fathoms deep); and Buduick mine may be visited, Polperro, Wheal Kitty, Wheal Alfred and others, most of them indicative of the arbitary names conferred on mines by the lively fancy of the Cornishmen. Population, 4,953.

Helston, taking its name from the marshy tract between it and the sea, is a parliamentary borough, but not otherwise remarkable. Meneage was the old name for the corner of Cornwall (down to the Lizard). It has good pasture, and a breed of small moorland horses. The Goonhills Downs run through the middle. *Wallowwarren*, the seat of Sir R. Vyvyan, Bart., is near to Marogan's old church. The metal Titanium was first discovered at Manaccan on Helford Creek. St Keverne was the birth-place of Incledon, the singer. Off the coast are the Manacle Rocks. The

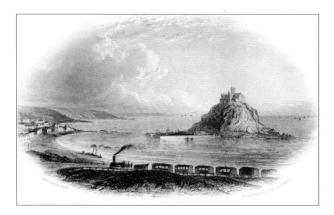

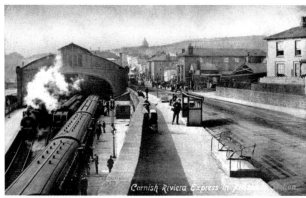

Cornish Riviera Express in Penzance Station

"Through the Window"
PADDINGTON to PENZANCE
GREAT WESTERN RAILWAY
PRICE · ONE SHILLING

Penzance
Above: This GWR publication from the 1920s features the distinctive St Michael's Mount. Originally the line rode into the Penzance along the sea front on one of Brunel's wooden viaducts, shown top left.

The North Cornish Coast
The harbour at St Ives, lower left, and Bude's Compass Point, shown below. According to the guidebook, this small port had 'within the last dozen years, risen to the dignity of a fashionable marine resort'.
(LoC)

St. Ives Harbour.

cliffs here are serpentine, soapstone, etc., covered with a profusion of heath, and extend past Black Head to the Lizard. This headland, which homeward bound ships from the westward always try to get sight of, is 18 miles from Penzance, and low, but pointed, whence the ancient name, Ocrinium, a corruption of Acritum. A little north-west of it is Kynance Cove, a place frequently visited by parties, on account of its high serpentine and soapstone cliffs, which exhibit the most beautiful colours, and contains little veins of minerals and spars. Vases and other ornaments are made from this stone. Population, 3,843.

PENZANCE

A telegraph station. HOTELS – Union; Star. MARKET DAYS – Thursday and Saturday. FAIRS – Thursday before Advent, Thursday after Trinity Sunday, and Corpus Christi day. BANKERS – Bolithos, Sons & Co.; Batten, Carne & Co.

This nourishing port is at the farther end of Cornwall, on the west side of Mount's Bay, at the terminus of the West Cornwall Railway. It is a municipal, but not a parliamentary borough, with a population of 9,414. Tin, copper, china, clay, granite, and pilchards, are the principal articles of trade here. The harbour, enclosed by a pier, 600 feet long, is shallow, but it is easy to reach and get out of. All the best shops are in the Market Place, where the four principal streets centre. The stannary court for the hundred of Penwith is abolished. An excellent Geological Society was founded in 1813; and is enriched by a full collection of specimens obtained by Dr Boase, from every corner of the county, and carefully arranged. The churches and houses are of stone. Madron is the mother church. Sir Humphrey Davy, the great chemist, was born at Penzance, 1778; after serving his apprenticeship to a chemist here, he went to assist Dr Beddoes at the Pneumatic Institution. Penzance is a cheap and healthy place for a resident. The soil in the neighbourhood is light and rich, from the granite dust at the bottom, and produces uncommonly heavy crops of potatoes, the returns being 300 to 600 bushels an acre. Sand, shells, and pilchards, are used to manure it. Mount's Bay, which is spread out before the town, is 18 miles wide at the mouth, from the Lizard Point on the east, to the Rundlestone on the west side. The shore is low and uninteresting; but what geologists call raised beaches are seen. St Michael's Mount, the most striking object in it, and to which it owes its name, is a conspicuous granite rock, four miles east of Penzance, about a quarter of a mile from the shore, off the town of Marazion. It is reached (at low water only) by a causeway, and stands 250 feet high. A few fishermen's cottages are round the base, and at the top are remains of a priory, founded before the Conquest, and for ages resorted to by pilgrims, whose rock is at the end of the causeway. Here the wife of the Pretender, Perkin Warbeck, found refuge in 1497. There are traces of a great variety of minerals; and it commands by far the best prospect of the bay. In olden times it was called Ictes, and was a tin depot. The flow of pilgrims to this point was the making of Marazion, which formerly possessed a good trade, but is now an insignificant town. Marghasion is its Cornish name, indicative probably of its position, and its being once held by Sion Abbey. Sometimes it is called Market-Jew, which is a corruption of another Cornish name, Marghasjewe.

Penzance is between the two districts which hem in the opposite sides of the bay, and form the tail end, as it were, of Cornwall, Kerrien towards the Lizard, and Penwith to the Land's End. Both possess a coast not very lofty, but broken and dangerous. They differ in their geological character – the Lizard district being mostly slaty or 'killas', and serpentine; and that of the Penwith, round the Land's End, granite, here called moorstone. Penwith signifies, in the expressive old British language, the 'point to the left', as it looks like a tract almost cut off from the main land. It is much the richest in minerals; though at one time Kerrien was remarkable for its produce in this respect. The surface of both is a heathy moorland, with little pleasant hollows here and there. In Penwith, eight or ten miles from Penzance, are the following places: The Guskus Mine, near St Hilary; Wheal Darlington Mine, near Penzance; and the Alfred Mine, near Hayle. Wheal (or Huel) is the common name for a mine, and synonymous with the English Wheel into which, being worked on the joint stock or 'cost book' system, every shareholder puts a spoke, all directed to one centre. *Trereiffe* is the seat of the Le Griees; *Trengwainton*, of Mr Davy. Near Ludgvan, (which was the rectory of Borlase, the county historian), is a large camp, 145 yards across. In the neighbourhood of Madron, or Maddern, are a pillar stone or two, and Lanyon Cromlech, which consists of a top stone or 'quoet', nearly 50 feet girth, resting on four other stones. St Buryan Church is a granite building, on point of the moorland, 47 feet high; it was once collegiate, and first founded by King Athelstane. Here, too, are various curiosities, as the Merry Maidens, Boscawen-Oen, the Pipers, etc., generally styled 'Druid', but in many cases the result of natural causes. A Cromlech at Boskenna, near the Camp and Lamorna Cave. Boscawen-Oon is a circle of nineteen stones, near the church, and gives name to the family of the Earl of Falmouth, one of whose members was the famous admiral. St Levan is close to a wild part of the coast. A little distance to the east is Treeren-Dinas, a camp in which stands the best Logan Stone (rocking stone) in Cornwall; it weighs 90 tons, but it is moved with a touch. One day in 1824 it was overturned by Lieutenant Goldsmith and his crew, in consequence of a bet; but the people round were so highly indignant that he was compelled to replace it, which he did in a very ingenious manner, having, at the instance of Davies Gilbert, Esq., the President of the Royal Society, obtained help from the Plymouth Dockyard. Tel Peden Penwith, as the extreme south point of the hundred is called, has a vast hole in the granite cliffs, through which the sea dashes up with a tremendous roar. A dangerous rock called the Rundlestone lies about one mile off it, marked by a buoy; and the dark Wolf-rock further out. The effects of the Atlantic and the weather upon the hardest rocks (as granite is supposed to be) are visible all along this broken and disintegrated coast – a wild desolate region to the eye, but extremely healthful and inspiriting. Rare shells, sea weeds, and plants, should be looked for. The Land's End, the ancient Antivestaeum, is in St Sennen, the most westerly parish in England - being, in fact, in a line with Dublin and the Western Islands of Scotland. On one side of the village signpost is inscribed, 'The first Inn in England' (if you come from the west), and the other, 'The last Inn in England'. Sweetbrier grows here wild. Sennen Cove is a lithe creek in Whitsand Bay. Longships Reefs, half a mile long, has a lighthouse on it, 83 feet high. Some miles out are the Seven Stones light vessels.

About 25 miles south-west are the Scilly Islands, a group of fifty or sixty granite islands and reefs, with an industrious population of 2,594. They belong to the Godolphin family. St Mary's the largest. Here Sir Cloudesley Shovel and four ships with 2,000 men were wrecked in a dreadful storm in 1707. A lighthouse has been fixed on St Agnes since this fearful event. Formerly there were fewer islands than at present, and it is said that a vast tract between them and the mainland was overwhelmed many centuries ago. That there is some truth in these traditions is evident, from what we see going on at the present time.

ST IVES ROAD

Telegraph Station at Hoyle, 1¼ mile.

The town of St Ives has a population of 10,353, chiefly depending on the coasting trade and pilchard fiehery. *Treganna Castle*, the seat of Mr Stephens, occupies a lofty situation outside the town, and, commands an extensive prospect.

MARAZION ROAD station.

BUDE. A small port and picturesque village in the north-eastern extremity of Cornwall – has within the last half-dozen years, risen to the dignity of a fashionable marine resort, to which distinction the excellent facilities it affords to bathers, and the picturesque scenery of its environs, have in a great measure contributed. The bed of the harbour, which is dry at low water, is composed of a fine bright yellow sand, chiefly consisting of small shells. The sea view is of a striking, bold, and sublime description – the rocks rising on every side to lofty broken elevations; and these who desire a sequestered and romantic retreat will find in Bude the very object of their wish. The Bude Canal was commenced in 1819, and completed in 1826, at a cost of £128,000. It terminates within three miles of Launceston, forming an internal communication through Devon and Cornwall of nearly forty miles. Bude is fifty-two miles from Exeter.

The Exeter and Exmouth railway is now open, and runs via the stations of TOPSHAM, WOODBURN ROAD, and LYMPSTONE. The route here described, however, is by the old coach road, which, by the lover of the picturesque and the still lingering fascinations connected with the old mode of travelling, may have its superior attractions. Passing through Topsham the road is studded with those charming old-fashioned villages that still linger in all their primitive simplicity along the western coast. From a hill called Beacon Hill, encountered in the progress, the eye is presented with a line of coast extending from Exeter to the southern boundary of Torbay, Berry Head, a distance of about twenty miles. This line is broken by several hills that ascend gradually from the opposite side of the river, clad with verdure to the summit, and sheltering the little village of Starcross in a wooded enclosure beneath. *Mamhead* and *Powderham Castle*, the seat of the Earl of Devon, heighten the beauty of the prospect, which is additionally embellished by the noble buildings connected with those estates.

Above: Ilfracombe, shown top, and looking north on Weston's sands. *Below:* Lynton's Castle Rock. Bradshaw struggled to describe the area's wild and beautiful scenery.

North Devon and Somerset

BARNSTAPLE

A telegraph station. HOTELS – Fortescue Arms; Golden Lion.
MARKET DAY – Friday. FAIR – Sept 19th. BANKERS – Drake, Gribble & Co.;
Branch of West of England and South Wales District Bank; National Provincial
Bank of England.

This sea port town is situated on the river Taw, which is crossed by a bridge of
sixteen arches. It first became a chartered town in the reign of Edward I, and was
formerly surrounded by walls, and defended by a castle. It had also the privilege of
a city and a harbour. The streets are well paved, and the houses built of stone. The
principal manufactures are baise and woolens, chiefly for the Plymouth market. It
has also a trade in bobbin net, paper, pottery, tanning, malt, and shipbuilding. Its
population is 10,743.

ILFRACOMBE

Telegraph station at Barnstaple, 11 miles. HOTELS – The Clarence, situated at
the higher end – and the Britannia and Packet Hotels, at the lower end of the
town. There is a boarding house on the quay, and excellent private lodgings in
every part of the town. MARKET DAYS – Saturday, for meat, poultry eggs, and
vegetables. FAIRS – One in April, the other in August.
BANKERS – Branch of the National Provincial Bank, and also of the Devon &
Exeter Savings Bank.

ILFRACOMBE is a considerable port town, and now a fashionable watering place,
on the north coast of Devon, near the mouth of the Bristol Channel. The harbour is
considered the safest and most convenient along the whole coast. It is formed like a
natural basin, and is almost surrounded by craggy heights that are overspread with
foliage. The town is built partly at the bottom of a steep declivity, and partly up the
side of it. New buildings and streets have been built, to afford accommodation to
visitors. The terraces and public rooms, forming the centre of Coronation Terrace,
have been constructed – the hot and cold baths at Crewkhorne have been formed,
and a number of new houses erected on the eastern side, commanding an extensive
prospect over the town and Bristol Channel to the Welsh coast.
BATHS – The direct way to Crewkhorne is by North-field to the baths, and
through the tunnel.
WALKS AND RIDES – The walks in this neighbourhood are very beautiful, and
afford delightful excursions and views.
Lynton and Lynmouth. The scenery in the neighbourhood of these two places
is 'wild and beautiful – magnificent and lovely' to use the words of a handbook of

Devon – the writer of which observes that it is quite beyond his powers to attempt a description of the scenery abounding in this fascinating neighbourhood. The accommodations for visitors are pretty nearly equal in each.

LYNTON HOTELS – Valley of the Rocks Hotel; the Castle Hotel; Crown Inn.

LYNMOUTH – An excellent inn called the Lyndale Hotel.

There are in both places lodging houses innumerable. The tourist should proceed to the far-famed Valley of the Rocks on foot, along the Cliff Walk, whence the scenery is very fine. The view in the valley is exceedingly grand. The East and West Lyn Valleys are very beautiful also; but the tourist should employ a guide to accompany him on his first visit to these and other principal points of attraction in this picturesque neighbourhood.

FREMINGTON and INSTOW stations.

SOMERSET

Few of the English counties present so great a variety of scenery and soil as Somerset. It possesses every gradation, from the lofty mountain and barren moor to the rich and cultivated vale, and then descends to the unimprovable marsh and fens. From Taunton to the coast extends a range of hills which slope towards Bridgewater, and on the other side they descend into a cultivated vale. Westward of this, and only terminating in the wild district of Exmoor Forest, the county is entirely mountainous and hilly. Between these there are many steep vallies, which form, when richly wooded, some of the most striking features of the beautiful scenery for winch this coast is so dosesrvedly celebrated.

Somerset, from its favourable climate and soil, stands very high in reputation for agricultural and rural produce.

BURNHAM

A telegraph station.

This place from its invigorating atmosphere and affording, as it does, the usual requisites of a sea-side retreat, has become valuable to the tourist in the summer season. Steamers run regularly, plying between this place and Cardiff.

WESTON-SUPER-MARE

Distance from station 2 miles. A telegraph station. HOTEL – Bath.

WESTON-SUPER-MARE has the advantage of being very accessible from Bristol, Bath, Exeter, and other towns on the line of the Great Western Railway, it has none of the picturesqueness arising from old streets and buildings, but, situated on the margin of Uphill Bay, near the Bristol Channel, it possesses the usual attractions of a neat watering place, having within the last ten years become considerably enlarged and frequented. The receding of the tide leaves a disfiguring bank of mud along the beach, which is a great drawback to the enjoyment of bathing; but a good market, numerous shops, and a delightful neighbourhood for rambling, present some counterbalancing advantages. Worle Hill is one of the pleasantest spots that a tourist could desire to meet with. In traversing the northern or sea side of the hill, the path lies, most of the way, through a copse of young fir trees, presenting occasional openings of the Channel and the rocky coast beyond. Towards the eastern end of the hill beautiful prospects are unfolded over a large and richly cultivated plain, extending to Woodspring Priory and Clevedon, with two or three churches standing up amid the elms and ashes. The nearest of these is Kewstoke Church, situated on the slope of Worle Hill itself. It derives its name from St Kew, who once formed his cell on the bleak hill top. From the church a craggy track, called the Pass of St Kew, consisting of a hundred natural and artificial steps, leads over the hill to the village of Milton on the opposite side, and these are said to have been worn by the feet of the pious recluse, as he daily went to perform his devotions at the church, which then occupied the same spot as it does at present. The ruins of the Priory at Woodspring are of considerable extent, and very picturesque, situated in a very solitary position at the farther end of a wide marshy but cultivated flat; they are divided from the sea by a narrow ridge of rocks, called Swallow Cliffs, quite out of the way of any frequented road. Crossing the broad mossy top of Worle Hill we can descend upon the village or Worle, which is prettily situated on the southern slope of the hill, and commands a delightful view over the richly cultivated flat to the range of the Mendip Hills. In short, the inducements to prolong a visit to Weston will be found principally to arise from the charming localities by which it is surrounded. The climate is bracing, and the air is very salubrious,

CLEVEDON

A telegraph station. HOTELS – Bristol, Royal.

This is a charmingly situated and rapidly improving watering place, much frequented by the citizens of Bristol during the summer season. Situated on the margin of the Bristol Channel, with rugged and precipitous rocks rising boldly up from the 'Deep waters of the dark blue sea'. Clevedon presents a very attractive place of resort to both the occasional tourist and valetudinarian, who seeks a quiet retreat for health's sake. Myrtles and other delicate shrubs flourish in the gardens at all seasons, so temperate is the air.

Wales – West Coast
Above, top: Barmouth,
showing the long
railway viaduct.
Middle: Llandudno

The North Coast
Left: Colwyn Bay's
Victoria Pier was
officially opened
in June 1900 and
later extended. The
imposing pavilion was
destroyed by fire in
1922 and again in 1933.

Wales

ABERYSTWYTH, on the coast of Cardiganshire, situated on a bold eminence, overhanging the sea, at the junction of the Ystwith and the Rhydol. The castle – its chief lion – was built by Gilbert de Strongbow, in the reign of Henry I, and now a mere ruin, is throned upon a projection of slate rock, protecting the town on the sea side, while on the other it commands the entire estuary of the two rivers, meeting at their point of confluence. Northward of the castle is a level beach, some hundred yards in length, to which succeeds a long range of slate rocks, worn into caverns and recesses by the dashing of the waves. Among the ruins is the favourite promenade, which, from its elevation, commands a magnificent view of the whole line of coast the forms Cardigan Bay. Nearly in the middle of this bay Aberystwith is seated, whence may be seen to the north a long irregular line, formed at first by the projecting coast of Merioneth, and then continued out to sea by the long mountainous promontory of Carnarvon, terminated by the Isle of Bardsey. There is no station southward of Carnarvonshire from which the Welsh Alps may be so advantageously seen as from Aberystwith Castle, or some of the surrounding cliffs. The lofty hills which bound the estuary of the Dovey, and raise their broad backs far above the Cardigan rocks, are surmounted by Cader Idris and its subject cliffs. These are overtopped by the giant mountains of Carnarvonshire, among which, in clear weather, the sharp peak of Snowdon itself may be discerned pre-eminent above the neighbouring crags. This wide expanse of water, diversified by numerous steamers and vessels in every direction – some steaming out for different ports in the bay, some further out at sea, and slowly shaping their course for Liverpool, Bristol, or Irish havens, while others, almost stationary, are busily employed in fishing – affording a varied and pleasant panorama of marine scenery; Pont ar Fynach, or the Devil's Bridge, is not more than twelve miles distant. A small portion of the Aberystwith & Welsh Coast Railway beyond Machynlleth is now open. It extends through GLYN-DOVEY and YNYS-LAS to BORTH, on the coast of Cardigan about 8 miles short of Aberystwith.

TOWYN, a thoroughly Welsh town, and a most rural watering place. St Cadfan's Church will delight an antiquarian. Hence follow the mountain road, by the majestic Cader Idris, whose Cyclopean precipices are upheaved in our very path, to...

DOLGELLLY – Here it will be found necessary to have a guide for its exploration, unless you have an ordnance map. Nearly 3,000 feet high, its summit commands a moat extensive panoramic view, with Snowdon on one side, Wrekin on another, Plinlimmon to the South, and the Brecknockehire Beacons beyond. Dolgelley itself is a lovely place, and may be made the centre of many an interesting excursion.

BARMOUTH may be visited from this. Ten miles up the coast from Barmonth is Harlech, with its historical old ruined castle, from which Craig Ddrwg and the Rhinog Faur (upwards of 2,000 feet high) may be climbed, with every yard full of Druidical and British remains.

BANGOR

A telegraph station. HOTELS – The George (sea view), Bangor Ferry, Miss Roberts, is a first-class house, delightfully situated between Bangor and Menai Bridge, and is deservedly celebrated for its excellent arrangements. The British (sea view), W. Dew, a favorite establishment, highly spoken of for its arrangements and general management. It has one of the finest coffee-rooms in North Wales. The Penrhyn Arms (sea view), Charles Bicknell, is a first-class establishment for families and gentlemen, and, from the high standing it has maintained for a series of years, may with confidence be recommended.

MARKET DAY – Friday. FAIRS – April 5th June 24th, September 16th, and October 28th.

A cathedral town and bathing place in Carnarvornshire, North Wales, near Snowdon, and only 2¼ miles from the Britannia Bridge. You enter it by a tunnel 3,000 feet long. It is an excellent resting place, not only for the fine mountain scenery of this quarter, but for the Britannia and Menai Bridges, the Penrhyn Slate Quarries, Beaumaris Castle, and other excursions, by road, railway, and boat. More than 50,000 persons come here in the season, so that lodgings at such times are high and difficult to be had. About forty years ago there were only ninety houses, now there are 1,336, to a population of 6,738.

The 'city' is chiefly a long street, winding about under the rocks towards Garth Point, where there is the public promenade, besides a ferry over the Lavan Sands to Beaumaris, on the Anglesey side. The peaks round Snowdon, and the rocky headlands of Pennmaen Mawr and Orme's Head are in view.

Among the buildings are the Assembly Rooms, Shone's Library, County Dispensary, Glynne's Grammar School, and a small plain Cathedral with a low tower, not older than the 15th century – the former one having been burnt by Owen Gwyndwr or Glendower. It was originally founded by St Deiniol, as early as 550, whence Bangor claims to be the oldest diocese in Wales. The income is £4,000 per annum. This argument was used when there was a talk of suppressing it some years back. There are tombs of two Welsh princes, Gryfydd (or Griffith) ap Cynan and Owen Gwyndwr; and a new painted window placed here by Dean Cotton, through whose exertions the church has been restored. It is the parish church to the town, the service being in Welsh. In the library is the missal and anthem book of Bishop Anian, who held the see in Edward I's time. Another bishop was Hoadley, appointed by George I; he preached a sermon here from the text, 'My kingdom is not of this world', so displeasing to the high church party, that it gave rise to a long dispute-the celebrated Bangorian Controversy.

A British camp and part of a castle may be seen on two points, near Friar's School. Further south is *Vaenol*, of the late Assheton Smith, a mighty hunter in Hampshire, and owner of the Dinorwic Slate Quarries, under Snowdon. About 30,000 tons are annually sent down to Port Dinorwic by railway, and 1,000 hands employed. Opposite, on the Anglesea side, is *Plas Newydd*, the seat of the Marquis of Anglesea, for many months the residence of the Duchess of Kent and Princess Victoria. It has the Anglesea pillar, fixed on Waterloo day in 1816, with a cairn and an immense Druid cromlech. Anglesea was the last and most famous seat of Druid worship.

LLANDUDNO

Telegraph station at Conway, 3½ miles.

This delightful place has now become one of great importance as a summer resort. It is situated 3½ miles from Conway, on a promontory between the Bays of Conway and Llandudno. The water is very clear, and affords excellent bathing, and being protected on the north by the Great Orme's Head, the air is peculiarly salubrious. The old Church (dedicated to St Tudno) stands on the mountain side. A new church was erected about 1839; but this is found much too small for the increasing requirements of the bathing season. There is also a fine market, well supplied with fish, vegetables, and in fact everything calculated to render the comforts of a temporary sojourn complete.

The scenery around is most picturesque, particularly so from the promenade which skirts the outer margin of the top of the mountain; at a height of 676 feet. The views from this point are of the most fascinating character. The town itself is in the very heart of the most attractive parts of North Wales. It can boast of some good water excursions, embracing some curious and picturesque caves both on the Great and Little Orme's Head.

RHYL

A telegraph station. HOTELS – The Mostyn Arms; the Royal; Belvoir; George; Queen's. MARKET DAY – Tuesday. Supplied profusely every day in the season.

RHYL, is a fashionable watering place for the North Wallians and Liverpool people; it is reputed one of the best bathing places in Wales. The beauty of the scenery, salubrity of the air, and firmness of the sand, render it a place of considerable attraction to visitors tram all parts of the kingdom. It is situated at the entrance of the celebrated vale of Clwyd, which extends twenty miles in length, and about ten miles in breadth, flanked on both sides with elevated hills. Snowdon can be seen.

In addition to the Hotels and Inns there are hundreds of elegant and respectable Lodging Houses, capable of affording excellent accommodation for visitors, at very moderate charges. These are bathing establishments and machines in abundance.

On the left of Rhyl are the celebrated range of British Posts, on the Clwydian Hills; established as a bulwark against an invading enemy.

Morecambe

Left: Choppy seas and warm clothing in this view of the Central Pier, which opened in March 1869. The pavilion was destroyed by fire in 1933. While Blackpool attracted visitors predominantly from the Lancashire mill towns, Morecambe's rail connections with Yorkshire and Scotland saw more holiday-makers from those areas.

Blackpool

Left: The electric tramway dates back to 1885 and is one of the oldest in the world.
Below: The town's most famous landmark, the tower, opened in 1894.

Blackpool's Luxury Rail Coaches.

Lancashire

A maritime county, situated on the north-western coast of England. This county includes part of the great coal fields of the north of England, and this circumstance, combined with its natural advantages for trade and manufactures, has gradually raised it to the rank of the greatest manufacturing county in the kingdom, containing Manchester, the centre of the cotton manufacture, and Liverpool, the great emporium of commerce for that side of our island. The soil and surface of the county are various; and its features in some parts, particularly towards the north, and all along its eastern border, are strongly marked. Here the hills are in general bold and lofty, and the valleys narrow and picturesque. On the sea-coast, and nearly the whole of the southern side of the county, following the course of the River Mersey, the land is low and flat. Moorlands are much more extensive than might have been expected in so populous a district, and where land is very valuable.

BLACKPOOL

A telegraph station. HOTELS – Rossall's; Clifton Arms; Albion; Lane End; Beach; Royal; Victoria; Brewer's.

This pretty bathing-place is situated on a range of cliffs fronting the Irish Sea. It takes its name from a pool near Vauxhall, the old seat of the Tildesleys, and contains a population of 3,506. This place is much frequented by visitors, and possesses an excellent Library, and sea bathing at all times of tide. The sea gains so much here that, on the Penny Stone 3¼ miles northward, and about a quarter of a mile from the shore, there formerly stood a small inn. Fine views of the Cumberland and Welsh hills, and the Isle of Man, can be obtained from several spots about here. In 1863 a new pier was opened, which forms a most pleasant promenade. During the season great facilities are offered for excursion to Furness Abbey, Ulverston, Coniston Lake, etc. In the vicinity is *Rake's Hall*, the seat of D. Horny, Esq.

A railway 7½ miles long now connects this place with Lytham. It runs along the South Shore, and affords great facilities to the public daily.

FLEETWOOD

POPULATION, 3,834. A telegraph station. HOTELS – Crown; Fleetwood Arms. STEAMERS to Belfast, daily (Sundays excepted), at or after 7½ p.m. Fares, 12s 6d and 4s. MARKET DAY – Friday.

FLEETWOOD, at the mouth of the Wyre, built on what was formerly a rabbit warren, is a modern town and port, which had no existence before 1836 but now contains a market, custom house, gas works: quay, 600 feet, a church, four chapels, etc., with a commodious harbour, from which steamers go to Belfast and the Lakes. The Light House is of iron screwed into the rock below the sand. In the vicinity is Rossall, a collegiate school for the sons of clergymen and others, with 250 pupils, and a full staff of masters. A steamer crosses Morecambe Bay, on week days, in summer, from Fleetwood to the Lakes district, at 10½ a.m., of which the nearest point is Piel.

MORECAMBE
Telegraph station at Lancaster, 3½ miles. HOTEL – North Western.

Morecambe station and harbour, from whence steamers sail, occasionally, daring the season, to Piel. Morecambe Bay is a fine sheet of water, 8 or 10 miles wide, when the tide is up; but at low tide its quicksands are extremely treacherous, and must on no account be crossed without the guide, who is paid by Government, and carries you over in a cart from Poulton-le-Sands, to the opposite coast of Furness – a region of fells, valleys, lakes, etc., in the north, but flat and broken by the sea, in the south or Lower Furness, where the beautiful remains of the Abbey may be visited. Near Dalton, Walney island light-house, and the old peel or tower of Foudray, built by the Abbots for a watch tower, are in view.

Retired from Sea.

EAST COAST BY L·N·E·R

LNER

Whitby
These traditional images of the town's fishing community, shown above, contrast sharply with the LNER poster's modernity.

84

Yorkshire

Which is a most important county, both as respects its topographical position and commercial advantages, returns six members. It extends 130 miles in length from east to west, and is 90 miles in breadth, from north to south; being not less than 460 miles in circumference. It is divided into three ridings, called the North, East, and West. The East forms the least of the three grand divisions of the county. Many parts of the wolds or hills in it afford magnificent prospects. From their northern edge the Vale of Derwent is seen extended like a map below, and beyond it the black moors towards Whitby rise in sublime grandeur. The western hills command an extensive view of the Vale of York, reaching far beyond that city into the West Riding. But the southern edge of the wolds is the most distinguished for the beauty and diversity of its prospects. The eastern portion of this elevated district skirting the Humber commands a most magnificent view of that vast estuary, extending to the southeast till it is lost in the horizon. It presents to the eye an interesting spectacle of numerous vessels floating to and from the port of Hull; while that opulent and commercial town, in its low situation, close to the banks, and surrounded by the masts of the shipping in the docks, seems to rise, like Venice, from amidst the sea; the whole composing a scene which, for beauty sad grandeur, can scarcely be exceeded.

WHITBY

POPULATION, 12,051. A telegraph station. HOTELS – Royal, on the West Cliff, for families and gentlemen; the Angel, family and commercial; Ward's Magnet; Commercial. MARKET DAY – Saturday. FAIRS – August 25th, Martinmas Day. RACES – In September, on the sands.
BANKERS – Branch of York City & County Banking Co.; Simpson & Co.

There are, among the watering places of England, few that have been more greatly benefited than Whitby from railway communication, or that have become better adapted for the reception of visitors. The town stands at the north east angle of the county of York, where the romantic River Esk pours its stream into the German Ocean. Enclosed between precipitous cliffs, the old town is scarcely to be seen, until nearly approached, though its locality is well pointed out by the ruins of its once stately abbey, which is still a beautiful object, adorning the east cliff; while on the west cliff, New Whitby, a magnificent pile of buildings, including a splendid hotel, recently built, containing warm baths, and every convenience for the accommodation of visitors, is admirably situated at an elevation of 100 feet above the level of the sea, commanding varied prospects, and at the same time accessible from the sands and the piers. Whitby has long been admired for the peculiarity of its position and the grandeur of its coast scenery. To the eastward the cliffs rise abruptly, nearly 200 feet above the sea, and towards the south present a succession of bold headlands. To the north the views along the coast are not less imposing. The headlands at Sandsend, Kettleness, Runswick, Staithes, Huntcliffe, and Rawcliffe, abrupt in outline, and varying in elevation from 200 to 600 feet, present a succession of coast scenery scarcely to be exceeded for beauty in England; whilst the valleys, opening up the country from the sea, are replete with picturesque beauty. The old church of St Mary stands close to the abbey, from which extensive prospects present themselves on every side. The ocean washing the beach, enlivened with passing vessels; the woods and castle of Mulgrave (the domain of the Marquis of Normanby); the piers, unequalled in this country for boldness of design; the town, harbour and swing bridge across the river, all immediately beneath the eye; the fertile valley of the Esk, the hills intersecting one another, villas, hamlets, plantations, and the moors beyond, covered with heath, altogether form a picture rarely surpassed. The west pier, extending 1,030 feet into the sea, with an elegant columnar lighthouse at its extremity, forms a favourite promenade; and the road cut through the solid rock and extending from the battery to the west cliff, is found to be highly advantageous to visitors.

There is probably no spot in England possessed of more varied rides and walks than the Whitby district. In every direction excursions may be formed: Robin Hood's Bay, Mulgrave Castle and woods, and the villages of Hawsker, Stainacre, Sneaton, Ugglebarnby, Alslaby, Sleights, Egton Bridge, Grosmont etc., are most accessible. Steamers are constantly plying to Scarborough, Redcar, Hartlepool, Stockton, etc., whilst sailing craft can be obtained at any hour to take trips in the offing. There is the usual accommodation provided for sea bathing. The beach extends three miles. Chambers the marine painter was a native. In the vicinity are *Whitby Abbey*, the seat of G. Cholmley, Esq., Lord of the Manor: *Airy Hill*, James Walken Esq.; *Low Stukesby*, John Chapman, Esq.; *Sneaton Castle*, the Rev. W. Giles; *Larport Hotel*, late E. Turtan, Esq.; *Hawsker Hall*, B. Gatliff, Esq.; and Robin Hood's Butts, distant six miles, 'the mark where Robin Hood's arrow flew when he shot before the Abbot of Whitby'.

SCARBOROUGH

POPULATION, 18,377. Distance from station, 1 mile. A telegraph station.
HOTEL – The Royal Hotel, for families and gentlemen; Crown, for families and gentlemen; Millhouses' Commercial and Family; Bull Inn, family and commercial. MARKET DAYS – Thursday and Saturday.
FAIRS – Holy Thursday, and November 22. RACES – In September.
BANKERS – Woodall & Co.; Branch of York City & County Banking Co.

SCARBOROUGH is undoubtedly the most interesting marine spa in England. With the advantages of mineral springs it combines those of a convenient sea-bathing shore, and on the land side it is surrounded by numerous objects of attraction, to which either roads, or footpaths over moors and dales, offer a ready access to visitors. Of its origin we have no satisfactory information, but its name has been most probably derived from the Saxon Scear, a rock, and Burgh, a fortified plane. No mention of it occurs in the Norman survey, but in the reign of Stephen we hear of the castle being erected, and doubtless that fortress soon became the nucleus of the town. Its situation is extremely beautiful and romantic, being in the recess of a fine open bay, on the coast of the North Sea, and the town consists of several spacious streets of handsome well-built houses, rising in successive tiers from the shore, in the form of an amphitheatre; the beach, of firm and smooth sand, slopes down gradually to the sea, and affords at all times that commodious open sea-bathing for which the place is so deservedly celebrated. From Robin Hood's Bay, northward, to Flamborough southward, there are thirty-three miles of coast, which may be inspected at low water, over a course of the finest sands in England, and which, with their caverns and promontories, rugged fissures and precipitous elevations, form a geological panorama of the greatest interest. Flamborough Head, with its lofty cliffs of nearly five hundred feet elevation, teeming in the timing and summer months with thousands of birds of every hue and species, and exhibiting yawning caverns of stupendous size – that called 'Robin Lyth Hole', being peculiarly noticeable – is of itself a promontory of unusual grandeur, and would be alone worth a pilgrimage from town. Not far distant either is Rievaulx Abbey, the beautiful ruins of which are presumed to indicate the first Cistercian monastery founded in Yorkshire, and which, in their magnificence of decay, are only surpassed by the famous Fountain's Abbey, that may be also brought within the compass of a summer day's ramble. In short, let the sojourn be ever so brief, the visitor will hence carry away with him a store of many memories of beauty, to which remembrance will afterwards recur with delight. To begin with one of these celebrities:

A fine terrace, one hundred feet above the level of the sands, forms a delightful marine promenade. The dissevered cliffs are connected by a handsome iron bridge of four arches, on stone pillars, in the chasm between which runs the stream called Millbeck. This bold undertaking, to afford facility of access to the spas, was completed in 1827, and its opening day was signalised by a bold charioteer, who, with four well-trained steeds in hand, drove a coach across the yet untested structure, amidst the acclamations of myriads, who covered the adjoining buildings and surrounding hills, all swarming with eager faces, intent on the hazardous performance of what appeared so perilous a feat. This bridge, which is one of the principal ornaments of the town is 414 feet in length and 75 feet in height, whilst the floor of the bridge is 14 wide, formed of transverse planks, and protected by an iron railing along each side. This airy fabric affords a view remarkably bold and striking, and far away beneath are the fine broad sands of the shore, where the Scarborough races are held, and where, says Dr Granville, in his happiest graphic vein, 'what at one hour was the estuary of living waters, murmuring in successive bow-like waves towards the foot of cliffs, becomes in the next hour, upon that occasion, the course-ground and the theatre of the equestrian as well as pedestrian display of man's skill and animal's agility'. The view of the horse-races from a place suspended in the air, and at such an immense altitude as this, is a sight only enjoyed, perhaps, by the people of Scarborough and the visitors to the Spa; for the cliff-bridge may be well described, on such an occasion, as the grandest stand of any in the world. Adjoining is the Museum, an elegant circular building,

Scarborough
Left: Scottish herring girls hard at work on the harbourside, *c.* 1905.

Staithes
Below: Picturesque beauty on the Yorkshire coastline.

for the display chiefly of British geological specimens, though possessing a fine collection besides of other rare and interesting objects, among which the skeleton of an ancient Briton and his oak-tree coffin, supposed to be 2,000 years old, will be found particularly attractive: the teeth are all perfect, and the skeleton would appear to have been preserved by the tannin, found dissolved by the water which had penetrated into the coffin. A very moderate monthly subscription will entitle the visitor to admission to the Museum, and as a pleasant lounge, fraught with interest and instruction, it may be considered a valuable addition to the general attractions of the town.

The mineral springs of Scarborough have been, for more than two centuries, held in the very highest repute. These springs are saline chalybeates, varying in the proportions of their several ingredients, and were for some time lost by the sinking, in 1737, of a large mass of the cliff; but, after a diligent search, they were recovered. The principal are the West and South Wells, situated at the base of the cliff south of the town, near the sea-shore, where a convenient building has been erected for the accommodation of visitors. The water of the south well contains 98 ounces, and that of the north well 100 ounces of carbonic acid gas in a gallon; the former is purgative, and the latter tonic. An elegant saloon in the building affords an opportunity for exercise in rainy weather; and being lighted by several windows facing the sea, the visitor has an opportunity of enjoying various picturesque views of the sea and coast. In a small sunken court, paved with flag-stones, and surrounded by stone walls, are the lion-mouthed spouts from which the water is continually pouring – the excess passing away through a small stone basin; and the substitution of this plan for the pumping up process usually adopted, imparts a zest and a freshness to the draught that invalids can thoroughly appreciate.

Fronting the sea are some net houses, let as lodgings, and called the 'Marine Houses'; they have a small adjoining building for cold and warm baths – the sea, at spring tides, reaching to nearly the threshold of its garden front. A lofty and sloping bank, from 150 to 200 feet high, thickly covered with shrubs and trees, rises hence, and goes to join the cliff bridge, in a southern direction, like a crescent bower. On the brow of this green embankment stand many of the best houses with a south or south-western aspect; and, on the sands below, a file of thirty or forty bathing machines, ranged on their broad wheels, stand ready for use. The gradual declivity of the shore, the softness of the sand, and the peculiar transparency and purity or the returning tide upon these open bays, render sea-bathing here not only perfectly safe, but absolutely luxurious. The town is supplied with fresh water by means of a reservoir holding 4,000 hogsheads, and being derived from land-springs is somewhat hard, but clear and wholesome to the eye and palate – an advantage few watering-places possess.

The harbour, easy of access, and safe and commodious within, is protected by two piers; one of them having been found insufficient to prevent the accumulation of sand, a new one was constructed, designed by Smeaton, the celebrated engineer. The breadth of its foundation is sixty feet; and at the curvature, where it is most subject to the action of the waves, sixty-three feet; it is forty feet high, and 1,200 feet in length.

The church, dedicated to St Mary, was anciently the conventual church of the Cistercian Monastery, and was formerly a spacious and magnificent cruciform building, with three noble towers; it sustained considerable damage in the siege of the castle in the time of the Parliamentary war, and retains but few portions of its ancient character the present steeple stands at the eastern end. Christ Church, a handsome edifice in the later style of English architecture, was erected in 1818, at a cost of £8,000. Other places of worship, and numerous hospitals and infirmaries, are scattered through the town. To the north of St Sepulchre's Street are the remains of a Franciscan convent, supposed to have been founded about the 29th of Henry III, and now used as a workshop.

The season may be reckoned to begin on the first of July, and terminate about the middle of October. During this period, houses and apartments can only be had at high prices; but, after the latter date, a residence may be obtained at half the amount. The railway, as in other instances, has materially increased the influx of visitors, and now new streets are being rapidly formed, to provide additional houses for their reception.

By a walk to the summit of Mount Oliver, or Oliver's Mount, from a tradition connected with Oliver Cromwell, a most superb panorama of land and water is to be enjoyed from a terrace 600 feet above the ocean, and these, together with excursions to the environs, which include much picturesque scenery, form the especial attractions of the strangers.

The climate of Scarborough is considered by Dr Granville to be extremely favourable, and the longevity of the inhabitants over those of other parts of Yorkshire is fully established. From its exposure on the east coast a mistaken notion is entertained by many that winds in an easterly direction must be of longer continuance at Scarborough than elsewhere; but this experience has shown to be an unnecessary fear. The mean average temperature in the month of January was found to be higher by six degrees than at York, four degrees than in London, and only two degrees less than at Torquay. In respect of climate, therefore, this 'Queen of Watering Places' affords immense advantages to invalids in the northern counties, who are unable to endure the fatigue of long journeys; and it is seldom that the sanitary effects of the sojourn, and the potent curative agency of the spas, are without their due influence in promoting and perfecting a return to health.

We now advert to the first object that strikes the eye of the visitor as he enters the town, but which we have reserved to the last, in order to give it that fullness of detail which its venerable ruins warrant. Scarborough Castle crowns a precipitous rock, whose eastern termination, which advances into the sea, rises about 800 feet above the waters. The principal part of the ancient castle now remaining stands at a considerable distance back from this bold and inaccessible front, but on ground which is nearly as elevated. It is a huge square tower, still nearly 100 feet high, but the walls of which show, by their ragged summit and other indications, that its original height must have been considerably greater. Each side is between fifty and sixty feet in length; but the walls being about twelve feet thick contract the space in the interior to only thirty feet square. This tower was probably the keep of the ancient castle; and, as usual, has been preserved from destruction by its extraordinary solidity and strength. As this old feudal stronghold looks down upon the sea on one side, it has the town of Scarborough stretched below it, and around it on the other, and imparts a bold and romantic aspect to the eastern extremity of the town.

The castle was built about the year 1136, by William, Earl of Albemarle, one of the most powerful of the old Norman nobility, and who was thus permitted by King Stephen to ensconce himself in the fortress, as a defence against the turbulent and but half-subdued inhabitants of the district. No situation could possibly have been chosen better adapted for defence; and, in the infancy of the art of warfare, it must have been absolutely impregnable. Within the boundary of its walls was once comprised an area of twenty acres; and what was of the greatest importance to the besieged, a spring of excellent water, that never failed its supplies even in the driest summer.

Norfolk, Suffolk & Essex

NORFOLK

This county, from its numerous objects of antiquity, geographical situation on the German Ocean, as well as its seaport towns, seats, agricultural and manufacturing products, is particularly deserving of notice. In the fenny part of the country the air is not only cold, but exceedingly damp; but the county to the north and north-west of Thetford, forming the greater part of Norfolk, consisting of a sandy or gravelly soil, is peculiarly salubrious and pleasant. The manufactures of Norfolk, which consist almost exclusively of woollen goods, are nearly all centred in the city of Norwich and its vicinity. Yarmouth and Lynn are the two principal ports, from which nearly all the manufactured goods are exported.

YARMOUTH

A telegraph station. HOTEL – Angel. STEAM VESSELS to Hull every Tuesday. Fares, 8s and 5s; to London, twice weekly. Fares, 8s and 5s; to Newcastle every Wednesday. Fares, 11s and 6s. MARKET DAY – Wednesday and Saturday. FAIRS – Easter Friday and Saturday. RACES in August. Marine Regatta in July or August. BANKERS – Gurneys & Co.; Lacon & Co. Branch of East of England Banking Co.; National Provincial Bank of England.

Below: Yarmouth's Britannia Pier, opened in 1858, repeatedly rebuilt, but still going strong. *(LoC)*

GREAT YARMOUTH is a seaport at the eastern extremity of the county of Norfolk, situate on the east bank of the Yare; the parliamentary borough extending on the west side with the county of Suffolk, comprising the hamlet of South Town and parish of Gorleston. Population, 34,810. It returns two members. The town stands on a tongue of land, having the sea on the east, and the river on the south and west, and joined to the mainland at Caister on the north. It is connected with South Town, by a very handsome lifting bridge (finished in 1854), constructed by Grissel & Co. The borough was incorporated by King John. In 1260 the town was surrounded (except on the river side) by a wall, having ten gates and sixteen towers, the remains of which are still to be seen. The town has, however, greatly extended itself beyond the walls. The Church, dedicated to St Nicholas, is one of the largest parish churches in the kingdom. It was founded in 1123, and has lately been restored. It contains a celebrated organ. Near it is the hall of the Benedictine Priory, restored and used as a school-room. The chief attraction of Yarmouth has always been its noble quay, extending upwards of a mile in length, and having for the most part admirable rows of trees, forming an agreeable promenade; adjoining to which are several Elizabethan houses, exhibiting rare specimens of carved work. The Town Hall and the Police Court are on the Quay. The Market Place is very spacious. There is a Theatre and a Public Library. On the beach a newly-erected Marine Drive extends (with the Victoria Terrace and Esplanade) for nearly a mile. At the south end, the Wellington (promenade landing) Pier, extends 700 feet from the terrace into the sea. At the northern extremity another pier is contemplated, and between them there is a free jetty near to which are the Bath Rooms Bathing machines placed both on the north and south beach.

The old town contains about 150 narrow street or passages, locally called 'Rows', extending free east to west, in which many remains of antiquity may still be traced. On the south Denes there is a column, 140 feet high, to the memory of Nelson. The inhabitants are chiefly engaged in the mackerel, herring, and deep-sea fisheries, which are here prosecuted to a very great extent with much success.

The Health of Towns Act has been introduced and the town is well drained, and supplied with an abundance of pure water from Ormesby Broad. In the immediate neighbourhood may be seen Burgh Castle, one of the most perfect Roman Camps in the kingdom; and the remains of Caister Castle which was erected by Sir John Fastolfe, K.G. temp, Henry VII. The town is defended seaward by three Batteries and it contains a Naval Hospital, and Barracks for the East Norfolk regiment of Militia, and the Norfolk Artillery Militia.

LOWESTOFT

Distance from station, mile. A telegraph station. HOTEL – Queen's Head.
MARKET DAY – Wednesday. FAIRS – May 12th, and October 10th.

A market and seaport town (the most eastern point in the kingdom), with a population of 10,663. It stands on a considerable eminence, commanding extensive views of the German Ocean and surrounding country. Its appearance from the

Above: The red-brown sails of herring fishing boats at Lowestoft's pierhead. *(LoC)*

sea is extremely picturesque. The town is neat, clean, and well lighted; contains Theatre, Assembly Rooms, Baths, and a fine church, dedicated to St Margaret, which should be visited, and its Porch, 'Maid's Chamber' over it, brasses, steeple and font should be noticed. In it are monuments to Bishop Scroope (brother to Bishop Tanner), Whiston Potter and Hudson, with the quaint epitaph 'Here lie your painful ministers, etc.', all of whom held that living. A chapel of ease, dedicated to St Peter, was erected a few years since by subscription. Admirals Usher, Ashby, Mighell (all natives), and Chief Justice Holt. Here, in 1665, the Duke of York defeated the Dutch Admiral Offdam. George II landed at this place in 1737, and Adams, the first American Ambassador in 1784. Admirals, Sir T. Allen and Sir Thomas Leake, Nash, the author, and Gillingwater, the historian, were natives. Harbour of Refuge, Tram Way, Promenade, Pier, Light Houses, Warehouses, and Sea Wall were erected in 1848, by Sir S. M. Pete, Bart.

SUFFOLK

This county is level, compared with many of the other English ones. The highest land is in the west, where the great chalk ridge of this part of the kingdom extends from Haverhill by Bury, to Thetford in Norfolk. The climate is considered the driest in the kingdom. Suffolk is one of the best cultivated districts in England; besides its arable lands, it contains heaths, which are employed as extensive sheepwalks. Indeed, it may be called almost exclusively a farming county, agriculture being conducted on the most improved principles.

IPSWICH

A telegraph station. HOTELS – White Horse, Crown and Anchor.

MARKET DAYS – Tuesday and Saturday. FAIRS – First Tuesday in May, July 25, August 22, and September 25. RACES in July.

BANKERS – Bacon, Cobbold, & Co.; Alexander & Co.; National Provincial Bank of England.

Ipswich, a port, borough town, and capital of the county of Suffolk, has a population of 37,950, who return two members. It is built on the northern bank of the river Orwell, and when viewed in ascending the river has somewhat the appearance of a crescent. The streets are rather narrow and irregular, like those of most ancient towns, but they are all well paved and lighted. The houses are many of them handsome modern buildings; and the rest, though old are substantial, commodious, and many have gardens attached to them. At the corners of several streets are yet to be seen the remains of curious carved images, and several of the ancient houses are covered in profusion with this description of ornament.

It contains Town Hall, Corn Exchange, New Market, Custom House (with an old ducking-stool), Barracks, Baths, Theatre (here Garrick made his debut, in 1741, as Ahearn in *Oronooko*), Lunatic Asylum, Hospital, Public Library, Assembly Rooms, Mechanics' Institute, Race Stand, Old Malt Kiln (once Lord Curzon's residence), Grammar School (of which Jeremy Collier was master), thirteen churches; Wolsey's House, where he was born, in 1471, stands near St Nicholas. Sparrow's House, Christ's Hospital, Ransoms & Sim's Machine and Agricultural Implement Works, which cover 14 acres; Public Park, Arboretum, the old churches of St Lawrence, St Margaret, etc. Wolsey, Butler (physician to James I), Bishops Brownrigg and Laney, Dick, Mrs Reeve were natives. In 1848 a two storied house was removed 70 feet without injury, and in 1850 a large apricot tree was carried a mile off – *Sharp's British Gazetteer*. In the vicinity is the *Chauntry*, the seat of Sir Fitzroy Kelly, M.P.

Ipswich is favourably situated for commerce. Vessels of any burden can navigate the Orwell to the town itself where a wet dock of considerable magnitude has been constructed. Vessels are constantly passing from Ipswich to Harwich. They are fitted up for the accommodation of passengers, like the Gravesend boats at London. This excursion forms one of the amusements of the place, for the beauty of the scenery along the banks of the river, bordered on either side, almost the whole way, with gently rising hills, villas, and woods, renders the sail delightful.

HARWICH

A telegraph station. HOTELS – Three Cups; White Hart.

MARKET DAYS – Tuesday and Friday. FAIRS – May 1st and October 18th.

A sea-port, packet station, and borough town in the county of Essex, with a population of 5,070, who return two members. It is built on a peninsular point of land, close to where the rivers Stour and Orwell join the German Ocean; and from the number of maritime advantages which Harwich possesses, it has become a place of fashionable resort, especially as the scenery in its neighbourhood has

94

considerable beauty. The Stour and Orwell are both navigable for large vessels twelve miles above the town, the one to Ipswich, the other to Manningtree. In uniting at Harwich, these rivers form a large bay on the north and west of the town. Their joint waters then proceed southward, and fall into the sea about a mile below it, in a channel from two to three miles wide, according to the state of the tide, and in which the harbour is situated. The western bank of it is formed by the tongue of land which projects towards the north, and on width the town itself stands; the eastern bank is formed by a similar projection towards the south of the opposite coast of Suffolk, and between these two promontories the harbour is completely sheltered. It is of great extent, and forms, united to the bay, a road-stead for the largest ships. Harwich derives considerable profit from its shipping trade, fisheries, and annual visitors. It has hot, cold, and vapour baths, every accommodation for sea bathing, and a number of other sources of amusement. From this place Queen Isabella (1326), Edward III (1338 and 1340), William III, George I and II, sailed on their visits to France, Holland, and Hanover. Queen Charlotte and Louis XVIII first landed here; and from hence was embarked, in 1821, the body of that much abused princess, Queen Caroline, consort of George IV. In the vicinity is Dover Court, in the church of which is a tomb to Secretary Clarke, killed in 1666 in action against De Ruyter. Here was a miraculous crucifix (at least so it was stated to be), for burning which three men were hung in 1532. Captain Hewitt sailed in H.M. surveying brig *Fairy*, from this port, and was lost, with his crew, on 13th Nov. 1840, in a storm.

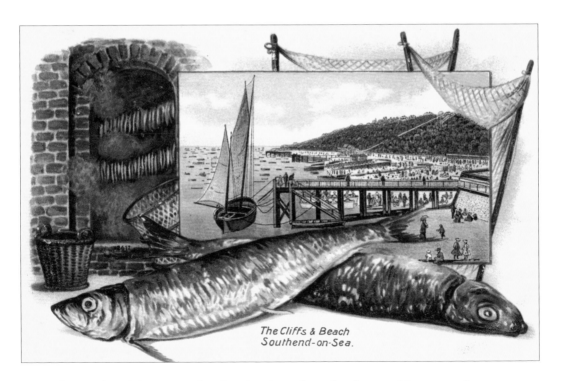

Above: Fish and ships at Southend-on-Sea. An embossed and eye-catching postcard, *c.* 1905.

ESSEX

SOUTHEND

A telegraph station. HOTELS – Ship, Chas. Woosnam,family and commercial hotel, a very comfortable house, and deservedly recommended; Royal Hotel, near the railway station.

A picturesque village in the county of Essex, situated at the mouth of the Thames, nearly opposite Sheerness. It has lately become known as awatering-place. Several handsome rows of houses have been erected, and bathing-machines established. The company that assemble here in the season will be found more select than at Margate, but it suffers severely in its climate when an easterly wind prevails. There are assembly rooms, theatre, library, a wooden terrace pier, 1,500 feet long, with a causeway 400 feet by 14 feet, which enables passengers to land at low water, and forms besides a pleasant promenade for those who love to enjoy the salubrity of the sea-breeze, and several places of worship. The view of the Thames from Southend is very pleasant, and the town is gradually rising in importance. It is situated on a wooded hill; and the beautiful terrace, commonly called New Southend, being built on a considerable eminence, gives the town an elegant appearance. The houses from this position command a delightful and extensive view of the sea, Nore, Medway, Sheerness, and the panoramic views of the shipping and steamers which are constantly passing up or down the river. The air generally is considered very dry and salubrious.

A final *Punch* cartoon – 'Finis! The End of the Season.'